D1682886

We Need Not Fail

Books by Sumner Welles

The Time For Decision

Where Are We Heading?

We Need Not Fail

SUMNER
WELLES

We Need Not Fail

Houghton Mifflin Company Boston
The Riverside Press Cambridge
1948

The Riverside Press
CAMBRIDGE · MASSACHUSETTS
PRINTED IN THE U.S.A.

Contents

Chronological Table

135 A.D. — Roman devastation of Palestine ends twelve hundred years of Jewish history in that land.

636 — Moslems under Omar occupy Holy Land.

1099 — The Crusaders under Godfrey de Bouillon capture Jerusalem.

1517 — Palestine conquered by Selim I, Sultan of the Ottoman Turks. Jews and Arabs live together under Turkish rule.

1917 — *November* 2. Balfour Declaration issued by British Government. Declares for a Jewish national homeland in Palestine.

1919 — *March* 3. President Wilson advocates a Jewish national state in Palestine.

1920 — Treaty of Sèvres — Turkey cedes Palestine to the Allies.
Mandate over Palestine given to Great Britain under League of Nations.
Mandate provides for establishment of Jewish homeland.

Austin denies right of Security Council to "enforce a political settlement." However, United States Government denies abandoning Partition.

March 18. President Truman assures Dr. Weizmann the United States has not changed its position.

March 19. United States Delegate announces to Security Council that his country requests abandonment of efforts to implement Partition and proposes Special Session of Assembly to consider a Trusteeship for Palestine.

April 13. Jews of Palestine announce they will establish an independent Jewish state on May 16, the day after the termination of the British mandate.

April 16. Special Session of General Assembly convenes.

April 17. Palestine Commission reports to Assembly that in light of Arab hostility, lack of British co-operation, and failure of United Nations to supply an armed force, it is impossible to implement the Partition resolution.

April 17. The Security Council demands that Jews and Arabs accept a truce. Unacceptable to Arabs unless Partition abandoned. Unacceptable to Jews unless Partition guaranteed.

April 20. United States proposes to Assembly a "temporary" Trusteeship, an elected legislature, subordination of Jewish immigration to an agreement between Jews and Arabs, relegation of policing of Palestine to members of United Nations capable of supplying and financing the armed forces required.

April 25. Russia demands a place on the Trusteeship Council.

May 14. At midnight, immediately upon termination of British mandate, the Jewish state of Israel proclaimed. United States at once gives *de facto* recognition to the new state.

Introduction

THE SHADOWS are lengthening. None of us can fail any longer to understand what the impending crisis signifies.

The new world order that took shape only three years ago at San Francisco, in which millions had placed their faith and their hopes, seems to be dissolving like mist before the sun.

The civilization of the West that has slowly and painfully struggled past the milestones of Magna Charta, Habeas Corpus, the American Constitution, "Liberty, Equality, Fraternity," and the Bill of Rights, is threatened with eclipse.

The peoples who have so often proved that they valued freedom more than life itself face the grim prospect that the same ideology which they believed had been forever crushed by their victory over the Axis, and which proclaims that the sole destiny of man is to serve a ruthless oligarchy, may yet, under a new guise, succeed in obliterating man's hard-won liberties from the face of the earth.

It would be foolhardy as these lines are written to attempt to prophesy what the world scene may be on the day they are published. But I write them with this underlying belief: the fate of Western Civilization will, for the time being, be determined by the course that our own country may adopt; by the ability of those in power in Washington to recognize the urgent need for vision, comprehension and courage, and, not least, by their capacity and willingness to learn from the lessons taught us by the past.

There is no question in my mind that peace can be preserved, that a free and lasting international order can still be fashioned out of the chaos of today, and that the principles of human liberty upon which Western Civilization rests can survive and can grow stronger in the years to come.

But it would be futile to anticipate any real start toward the attainment of those objectives – and time is fast running out – unless the American people see why some of the recent policies of their Government threaten the destruction of the one agency through which a better world can eventually be built. That agency is the United Nations.

Most of us recognize that in this atomic age Western Civilization cannot survive unless some form of workable collective security is soon established. The world cannot permanently be unified by any unilateral imposition of force. It can be unified by collective security under the rule of law and justice.

The League of Nations was the first practical experiment in collective security. It failed. It failed because the major Powers, blind to all save the appeal of selfish expediency, withheld from the League of Nations the power without which its authority could not be enforced. Selfish expediency prevailed when Japan invaded Manchuria in 1931. It prevailed when Hitler violated the Treaty of Versailles and reoccupied the Rhineland in

1936. It prevailed in 1938 when Hitler seized Austria and began the destruction of Czechoslovakia.

We face today exactly the same challenge. We face it not only in the case of Soviet expansion; we face it equally in the case of Palestine.

The General Assembly of the United Nations, under the powers granted it by the Charter, determined last November that the economic union of Palestine together with the creation within the Holy Land of two politically independent states was the solution most likely to safeguard the maintenance of world peace. The United States and the Soviet Union both supported that solution. No veto was employed in the Security Council to block the plan that the Assembly had adopted.

The Arab states, however, threatened to resist "by every means within their power" the implementation of this plan. When they saw that the United Nations could be defied with impunity, they resorted to armed aggression. They have invaded Palestine.

The United States has declared itself unwilling that the Security Council should enforce the will of the Assembly of the United Nations. It has proposed that the United Nations should abandon the decision it had reached. We are witnessing just such a precedent as that created when Japan invaded Manchuria in 1931: the refusal by a major Power for selfish reasons of alleged expediency to permit the United Nations to enforce its authority.

The results are already apparent. The Finnish Government, confronted with an ultimatum from the Soviet Union to sign a treaty of military alliance that will bring Finland behind the Iron Curtain, sadly announces that the United Nations has proved itself unable to protect "the small and the weak." In Western Europe those other democracies that find themselves in the front lines in this new world contest have seen that the United States is not only unwilling to grant the United Nations the authority it must have if it is ever to protect "the small and the weak," but equally unwilling to abide by its own commitments when these seem to involve unexpected risks and new burdens. Will their determination to resist Soviet aggression be thereby fortified?

Many who have seen the humanitarian issues, and the issues of justice, in this problem of Palestine, have failed also to see how large a part the decision upon the fate of Palestine must play in determining the future of the United Nations.

I have accepted my publisher's invitation to write this book because I believe that the nature of this decision will shape our own national destinies and the future of humanity.

The question of Palestine, alien to our national interests as many of us still believe it to be, affords a test of the capacity of the American people to attain those objectives – peace and freedom – for which they have sacrificed, fought and died in two World Wars. Let us not forget that in 1931 Manchuria seemed equally remote.

Arnold Toynbee, in *Civilization on Trial,* states the whole tremendous issue in these words: "Creation . . . wins its ultimate successes through a process of trial and error; and accordingly, the failure of previous experiments, far from dooming subsequent experiments to fail in their turn in the same way, actually offers them their opportunity of achieving success through the wisdom that can be gained from suffering. . . . As human beings, we are endowed with this freedom of choice, and we cannot shuffle off our responsibility on the shoulders of God or nature. We must shoulder it ourselves. It is up to us."

We Need Not Fail

1

What Is Palestine?

DURING RECENT MONTHS I have received several thousand letters which refer to Palestine. Many of their writers seem to ignore Palestine's recent history and to have no knowledge of the status of the Holy Land. This is typical of the opinion expressed in many of these letters: "There is no equity in the aggression represented in seizing land from peoples who have inhabited it for two thousand years, and turning it over to a set of invaders just because these are persecuted in Europe."

The author of the letter from which I have quoted is undoubtedly sincere. He believes that the establishment of a Jewish state in Palestine represents an act of grave injustice. But such charges as this certainly show a surprising unfamiliarity with the history of our own times.

The Roman devastation of Palestine in 135 A.D. ended some twelve hundred years of Jewish history in that land, with the slaughter or expulsion of most of the Jews. Palestine then became successively a part of the Roman and Byzantine Empires. Subsequently it was occupied for three centuries by the Arabs. After these were conquered by the Seljuk Turks, Palestine passed from the hands of one conqueror to those of another. For almost a hundred years after 1095 A.D. it was under the control of the Crusaders. But from the year 1517 A.D., when the Ottoman Turks conquered it, until the close of the First World War, Palestine was continuously a province of the Turkish Empire. Except for the Egyptians and some of the other peoples of North Africa, none of the present Arab nations obtained their freedom from Turkish rule until Turkey was defeated by the Allies in the First World War.

On August 10, 1920, the victorious Allies compelled Turkey to sign the peace treaty of Sèvres. By the terms of that treaty Turkey was forced to cede to the Allies her province of Palestine. Under international law Palestine thus became subject to whatever disposal the Allies might decide to make of its inhabitants and territory.

By common agreement, sovereign jurisdiction over Palestine, including the territory now known as Trans-Jordan, was vested by the Allies in the League of Nations. In 1920 the League granted a mandate over Palestine to Great Britain. In 1947 Great Britain notified the United Nations, as successor to the League of Nations, of her decision to terminate her mandate.

For the last thirty years the right to determine the destinies of Palestine has consequently been vested in the organized society of nations, first known as the League of Nations and now termed the United Nations. There is no valid ground upon which that right can be challenged. Nor is there any ground in law or in equity upon which the Arabs can base their claim to possess the right of sovereign jurisdiction over Palestine. Of the three thousand years that have passed since the Israelites first entered the Holy Land the Jews have been a dominant force in that region for some twelve hundred and the Arabs but some four hundred years. Since it became a Turkish province, Jews as well as Arabs have always inhabited Palestine. The Arabs never by their own efforts won their independence from Turkey. While the Holy Places are sacred to Jews, Moslems, and Christians alike, Palestine has never been the spiritual and historic Homeland of the Arabs as it has ever been that of the Jews.

In the light of these facts the charges that are made that the Jews who seek a haven in Palestine are "a set of invaders," or that a determination by the United Nations that the highest interests of both Jews and Arabs, as well as the cause of world peace, require the partition of Palestine is an act of "aggression," are as unfounded as they are absurd.

Mr. Lloyd George, long after he had ceased to be Prime Minister, once said to me that he was still being attacked by his opponents for his failure to secure greater territorial concessions for Great Britain at the Peace Conference of 1919. He protested, "They still are saying this even though I won for the Empire the mandate over Palestine." It must be admitted that during the years between the two Great Wars British policy frequently justified the general impression that Palestine had in fact become a British possession.

From the standpoint of Britain's imperial interests thirty years ago the mandate over Palestine was undeniably of prime importance. Palestine was a key to the control of Egypt and of the Red Sea, and of the British lines of communication to India and the Far East. The Port of Haifa afforded a strategic base in the Eastern Mediterranean. It was also the most advantageous outlet for the oil produced in Iraq.

Palestine possessed few natural resources. After centuries of neglect and of misrule it had become an arid or semi-desert region. It had an area of less than ten thousand square miles. Its total population before the First

World War was less than 700,000. Of its inhabitants about one quarter was composed equally of Jews and Christians. The remainder were Moslems, of whom a majority were migrant Bedouins. But her control over Palestine, apart from the territory's strategic significance, offered Britain two assets which, while intangible, were of no small value. By her assumption of the mandate Britain obtained sole charge of the Holy Places. She also was given the chance to win the lasting gratitude of the Jewish people were British rule to enable them to find once more within the Holy Land that national home of which they had so long been deprived.

During the many centuries of their exile Zion has been the ideal of innumerable devout Jews. It has been traditionally their spiritual aspiration. It has symbolized surcease from suffering and persecution. Only recently has this nostalgic longing for the Promised Land developed political aspects.

Early in the eighteen-nineties one of the recurrent epidemics of anti-Semitism afflicted Western Europe. The notorious Dreyfus case in France was one of its manifestations. Doctor Theodore Herzl, an Austrian Jew who was attending the Dreyfus trial as a newspaper reporter, there conceived of Zionism as we know it today. His propaganda made rapid headway. Prominent and wealthy Jews in many parts of Europe like the Rothschilds in Paris, or the Russians who organized as "The Lovers of Zion," began to finance the purchase of land in Palestine so that some of the more unfortunate members of their race might settle there. The international Zionist organization was founded in 1897 at a congress in Basel. Large contributions came from all over the world to establish a Jewish national fund to be used to increase land holdings in Palestine and to help needy Jewish settlers.

In Great Britain, which bears the honorable record of being a European nation where anti-Semitism has, until very recently, been long unknown, there was already before the First World War much popular sympathy for the Zionist cause. It was only natural that it should be a British Government from which Zionism received its first official support.

One of England's leading Zionists, and one of the greatest figures that Jewry has produced in modern times, is Doctor Chaim Weizmann. The help he gave the British Government during the First World War was invaluable.

His fellow Zionist, Lord Melchett, tells this story: "Working for the Admiralty Weizmann perfected his most subtle and complicated method of obtaining alcohol from wood at a time when this material, absolutely vital for the production of explosives, was becoming impossible to obtain in sufficient quantities owing to the submarine campaign and the abnormal conditions of war. Mr. Lloyd George has himself described the case and said that, confronted with one of the most serious crises with which he was ever beset in the Ministry of Munitions, we were saved by the brilliant scientific genius of Doctor Weizmann. Both he and the Allies felt a deep debt of gratitude, and when they talked to him and asked 'What can we do for you in the way of an honor?' he replied, 'All that I care for is the opportunity to do something for my people.' "

Britain's recognition of this debt of gratitude, and a spirit of idealism which has by no means infrequently influenced the British people, together with a more material motive, were all responsible for the official backing given by the British Government to the Zionists' appeal for their Homeland.

Arthur James Balfour, then Secretary of State for Foreign Affairs, who was a fervent believer in Zionism, became the spokesman for the British Cabinet of which David Lloyd George was Prime Minister.

The statement of official British policy, known as the Balfour Declaration, was issued on November 2, 1917:

> His Majesty's Government view with favor the establishment in Palestine of a national home for the Jewish people and will use their best endeavors to facilitate the achievement of that objective, it being understood that nothing should be done that may prejudice the rights of existing non-Jewish communities in Palestine or the rights and political status enjoyed by Jews in any other country.

The Balfour Declaration has been termed the Magna Charta of the Jewish people. Endorsed as it later was by the United States, and by all of the other Allied Powers, it was rightly regarded by the Jews as a solemn pledge that they would be helped to rebuild a Jewish nation in the home of their forefathers.

There has been much dispute as to the precise significance of the pledge given in the Balfour Declaration and particularly as to the meaning of the words "National Home." The answer to the question raised is to be found in the clarifications later given by members of the Lloyd George Cabinet which had issued the Balfour Declaration in the name of the British people.

Some years after the Declaration Mr. Lloyd George testified before a Royal Commission sent to Palestine to recommend a new administrative policy.

The Commission's report contains this record of his testimony:

> Mr. Lloyd George . . . stated that while the Zionist cause had been widely supported in Britain and America before November 1917, the launching of the Balfour Declaration at that time was "due to propagandist reasons"; and he out-

> lined the serious position in which the Allied and Associated Powers then were. The Rumanians had been crushed. The Russian Army was demoralized. The French Army was unable at the moment to take the offensive on a large scale. The Italians had suffered a great defeat at Caporetto. Millions of tons of British shipping had been sunk by German submarines. No American divisions were yet available in the trenches. In this critical situation it was believed that Jewish sympathy or the reverse would make a substantial difference one way or the other to the Allied cause. In particular Jewish sympathy would confirm the support of American Jewry, and would make it more difficult for Germany to reduce her military commitments and improve her economic position on the Western Front.

Mr. Lloyd George continued:

> The idea was, and this was the interpretation put upon it at the time, that a Jewish state was not to be set up immediately by the peace treaty without reference to the wishes of the majority of the inhabitants. On the other hand, it was contemplated that when the time arrived for according representative institutions to Palestine, if the Jews had meanwhile responded to the opportunity afforded them by the idea of a national home and had become a definite majority of the inhabitants, then Palestine would thus become a Jewish Commonwealth.

Since the Balfour Declaration was later incorporated into the mandate for Palestine granted by the League of Nations to Great Britain, the testimony of the man who was Prime Minister of the United Kingdom at the time the Declaration was issued, is necessarily conclusive. There is, however, much other similar authoritative evidence. Mr. Lloyd George's testimony makes it plain that the pledge in the Balfour Declaration was far from being merely a rhetorical assurance of sympathy for the aspirations of a great people. It was given, at a moment of great danger to the Allied cause, because of the value of the Jewish support that was anticipated as a consequence. It was in the nature of a compact.

A statement issued for the United States by President Woodrow Wilson on March 3, 1919, should also here be quoted: "I am persuaded that the Allied nations, with the fullest concurrence of our own Government and people, are agreed that in Palestine should be laid the foundations of a Jewish Commonwealth."

This announcement of the meaning attributed by the United States to the terms of the Balfour Declaration was later confirmed in several official acts of the executive and legislative branches of the American Government.

Soon after it had obtained the Palestine mandate the British Government demanded of the League of Nations a radical modification of the mandate's original scope. On September 16, 1922, the Council of the League decided to suspend those provisions of the mandate that related to the Jewish national home in their application to the eastern part of Palestine, known as Trans-Jordan. That territory, which was three and one-half times larger than the region now known as Palestine, was thereafter closed to Jewish immigration. Trans-Jordan was placed under a separate British mandate. Through British influence, and backed with a British subsidy, the Emir Abdullah became chief of the new state. Since the Second World War Trans-Jordan has become a sovereign kingdom; it has been recognized as independent in a treaty concluded with Great Britain, and it has applied for admission to the United Nations.

In 1920, Sir Herbert Samuel, himself a Jew, was sent by the British Government to Palestine as High Commissioner to carry out the administrative obligations that

Great Britain had accepted under the terms of the mandate. The High Commissioner was not a Zionist. From the outset, however, the Arabs in Palestine refused all co-operation with the British authorities, and rejected the mandate as invalid. While under subsequent High Commissioners there were periods of brief tranquillity, the history of British administration in Palestine is on the whole a record of continued controversy, of repeated hostilities between Jews and Arabs, of frequent uprisings against the mandatory power, and of constant vacillation in London as to the policy to be carried out. At times there has been considerable Jewish immigration. At other times it has been negligible. In 1931, for example, only 4075 Jews entered Palestine. After Hitler came to power, immigration rose so sharply that the total for the year 1935 amounted to 61,854.

Yet notwithstanding consistent Arab opposition, notwithstanding fluctuations in the current of immigration, and notwithstanding the lack of any constructive or even sympathetic policy on the part of the local British administration, Palestine little by little began to be to Jews throughout the world, an increasingly encouraging demonstration that the promised Homeland was no longer a mere dream. More than five hundred million dollars of Jewish capital was invested in the country. Farm communities founded and operated by the Jews sprang up in every part of the Holy Land. A race that had never been thought to have any special aptitude for agriculture developed within this exhausted and arid territory some of the richest agricultural centers of the world. New industries were established and prospered. A great and completely new city, Tel Aviv, was built by the Jews on desert land near the old port of Jaffa. Only thirteen years after the inauguration of the mandate, Palestine's imports from Great Britain amounted to more than fifteen millions of dollars, while an increasingly lucrative outlet for many Palestinian exports, notably tobacco and citrus fruits, was secured in many countries of Europe. Palestine began to be an important field for the investment of British capital, as distinguished from purely Jewish capital, and a steadily expanding market for British industrial goods.

As the economic strength of the Jewish Community developed, and as Jewish land holdings increased, the resentment of the Arab population grew in intensity. Yet, in many ways, the welfare of the Arabs had been materially enhanced by Jewish endeavors. Land values mounted steadily. Irrigation projects, financed by the Jews, necessarily benefited adjacent Arab farms. Health and sanitation projects helped Jews and Arabs alike. Living standards rose. The purchasing power of the Arab communities however, for lack of Arab initiative and enterprise, increased far less rapidly than that of the Jews. Friction between the two peoples eventually was transformed into open hostility. There was, unfortunately, no sign of any practical effort or of any serious desire on the part of the British authorities to find a way to alleviate the tension before it reached the danger point.

There were several reasons for this tragic failure in administration. There is little doubt that many anti-Zionists were appointed to key positions in the British administrative agencies in Palestine. It is equally true that when the administration of Palestine was placed under the jurisdiction of the British Colonial Office many of the permanent officials of that Department were strong in the belief that Palestine should eventually become a British Colony, and they consequently felt that any policy which might facilitate the creation of the national Jewish home envisaged in the mandate should be blocked. There were undoubtedly honorable exceptions. But a majority of the British civilian and military administrators in Palestine were representatives of the imperialist tradition of the nineteenth century. No form of sincere co-operation between the Jewish leaders of Palestine and the British Administration was usually possible.

Finally, the Baldwin, MacDonald, and Chamberlain Cabinets that held office between the two world wars showed no inclination to recognize either in spirit or in letter the pledges given to the Jews by the Lloyd George Cabinet. Yet during those years the gratitude of the Zionists to Great Britain was so deeply felt that even the ultra-Zionists wanted nothing better than a permanent alliance between Great Britain and the future Jewish Commonwealth. They supported with equal enthusiasm Colonel Josiah Wedgwood's proposal in the House of Commons that Palestine become a Dominion in the British Commonwealth of Nations.

For lack of a consistent British policy directed toward the redemption of the pledges given in the Balfour Declaration, and because the opposition of many individual British officials to the establishment of a Jewish Commonwealth often showed itself in open favoritism toward the Arabs, Arab antagonism finally flared out in concerted violence.

The first major crisis arose in 1936. It began with an Arab protest against any further immigration into Palestine of the Jews who were fleeing from Nazi Germany. In April of that year the Arabs called a general strike. Sporadic rioting soon turned into armed rebellion. Within a few months more than a thousand lives had been lost. A British Royal Commission, headed by Sir Arthur Peel, was dispatched from London to investigate the situation and to recommend the steps to be taken to halt conditions that gave every indication of fast becoming a state of open anarchy. The report rendered by this Commission was the most significant contribution toward a solution of the Palestine problem that was made before the Second World War.

Article 6 of the Palestine mandate contained this directive from the League of Nations to the British Government:

> The administration of Palestine, while insuring that the rights and position of other sections of the population are not prejudiced, shall facilitate Jewish immigration under suitable conditions, and shall encourage, in cooperation with the Jewish Agency referred to in Article 4, settlement by Jews on the land, including state lands and waste lands not required for public service.

The Peel Commission charged that Britain had largely disregarded this directive from the League. It declared that the British Administration had continuously placed obstacles in the way of future Jewish immigration, and had discouraged Jewish settlement on the land. According to the Commission the British authorities seemed to be doing nothing at all beyond trying to maintain some kind of tenuous balance between the Jews and Arabs.

As Mr. Lloyd George trenchantly put it in the House of Commons when the Commission's report came up for debate: "You are using the fact that you are doing nothing for the Arabs as an excuse for forbidding the Jews to do something for themselves."

The Commission complained that the British Administration had refused to employ qualified Jews in local government; it had imposed punitive taxes upon the machinery imported by Jews to be used in the creation of new industries; what was graver still, in several instances where Jewish settlements had been attacked by Arabs, the British had arrested the Jews who were trying, in default of official protection, to defend themselves, and had tried them on the same charges as their Arab aggressors.

The report of the Peel Commission bluntly declared that the British mandate in Palestine had failed.

It summarized its findings in these words: "The obligations Britain undertook toward the Arabs and the Jews some twenty years ago have proved irreconcilable. We cannot – in Palestine as it now is – both concede the Arab claim to self-government and secure the establishment of a Jewish national home."

The Commission therefore urged that Palestine be partitioned into two independent states, a Jewish state of scant territorial extent and a far larger Arab state. It recommended, however, that the British mandate should continue over the Holy Places and over such strategic seaports as Haifa.

The recommendations of the Peel Commission were rejected by both Jews and Arabs; by the latter because they refused to admit that the Jews had any rights; by the Jews because the meagre area allotted to them would have been too small to accommodate many more settlers, and because within its limits no viable independent state could have been established.

The Commission's findings were even more emphatically rejected by the British Government. Dominated as it then was by the most short-sighted and reactionary leaders that the British Conservative Party had produced in recent times, it disavowed its own Royal Commission.

A year later, in April 1938, the Chamberlain Cabinet sent out to Palestine another Royal Commission – the Woodhead Commission. The findings of this Commission were wholly negative. No constructive solution, let alone a permanent solution, was even envisaged. The Commission largely limited itself to the expression of its opinion that the atmosphere in Palestine was "charged with intense hatred and bitterness," and that "the tension between the Arab and Jewish communities was probably greater than it had ever been before."

The British Government itself had nothing better to propose than the device to which it has so often resorted before and since: consultation between Jewish and Arab leaders. At the round-table conferences in London in 1939, to which, in addition to Palestinian Arabs, delegates from the independent Arab states were invited, no progress was made. The consultation proved wholly abortive.

But the ensuing stalemate resulted in the violation by the British Government of its official pledges to the Jewish people and of its obligations as their Trustee under the League of Nations. The Chamberlain Cabinet welshed on its commitments on the ground that the international situation was so precarious that it could not risk Arab hostility. Its action is sadly reminiscent of the course of the United States nine years later.

The White Paper proclaimed by the British Government in 1939 flagrantly dishonored, in letter and in spirit, the Balfour Declaration and the terms under which the British had accepted their mandate.

The White Paper provided that from that time on no more than seventy-five thousand Jewish immigrants were to be permitted entrance into Palestine, and that after that total had been reached all further Jewish immigration was to be prohibited. And it must not be forgotten that this step was taken at the very moment when Palestine offered the one hope for survival of many of those

Jews in Central Europe whom Hitler had not yet liquidated!

This action of the British Government was followed by its open defiance of the League of Nations.

The League's Mandates Commission, which was similar to the present Trusteeship Council of the United Nations, possessed supreme authority over all the mandated areas. The Commission had already often remonstrated with the British Government for its failure to comply with the terms of its Palestine mandate. The White Paper necessarily brought on a crisis.

The Mandates Commission condemned the White Paper. It maintained that it "was not in accordance with the interpretation which, in agreement with the mandatory Power and the Council of the League of Nations, the Commission had always placed on the Palestine mandate."

The Mandates Commission comprised some of the most enlightened and courageous statesmen of that day, a majority of them representatives of the smaller Powers. The British Government ignored their opinion. It denied the right of the League of Nations to demand that a mandatory Power comply with the obligations it had assumed both to the League and to its wards.

Jewish immigration into Palestine was immediately restricted. All further Jewish land purchases were prohibited. While the Jews of Central Europe were fleeing for their lives, Great Britain closed the doors of Palestine.

During the nineteen years between the assumption by Great Britain of her Palestine mandate and the outbreak of the Second World War, the Jewish population of Palestine had risen to a total of some six hundred thousand souls, roughly one half of the Arab population. The Jews, during this brief span of time, had been responsible for a modern miracle. Their intensive cultivation of the soil, their rapid construction of new cities and towns, their establishment of new industries that provided employment for many thousands of immigrants, had within an incredibly short period brought into being a diversified and prosperous economy which had raised the living standards of all of Palestine's inhabitants – Jews, Arabs, and Christians alike. What the Jews had accomplished was invaluable as an example to the backward and impoverished peoples of the Arab world. The new country they were building promised to become a source of increasing wealth to all of the nations of the Near East.

It was now, when the new Palestine that they had created had also become the one hope for the future that still remained for so many members of their persecuted and tragically afflicted race, that the realization of their promised Homeland seemed suddenly once more unattainable.

2

Palestine During the Second World War

When the Second World War broke out, the chances for the establishment of a Jewish Commonwealth in the Holy Land seemed indeed to have vanished. Yet the forces that the war brought into being had a determining effect in arousing world public opinion to the imperative need of finding a solution for the Palestine problem. Political and military developments during the war, and the rise of a contest in power politics at the close of the war, both helped to bring on a crisis in Palestine whose implications, humanitarian, strategic and political, were much too far-reaching for any British Government to solve by its own unaided efforts.

Because our thinking about the Near East is often biased by our recollection of the romantic exploits during the First World War of Lawrence of Arabia, we are inclined to assume that the relations between Great Britain and the Arab peoples are peculiarly close and that the support the Arabs gave Britain and her Allies during the Second World War was as staunch as it had been a generation earlier. The reverse is, of course, the case.

There was a rapid growth of nationalism throughout

the Arab countries after 1920. The efforts of Great Britain to perpetuate a system of protectorates over the Arab kingdoms, and in particular over such advanced states as Egypt and Iraq, aroused among the younger Arabs a spirit of bitter hostility to Western imperialism. The brutal repression that France exercised in Syria and the Lebanon contributed perhaps even more to incline the "young Effendis" and other intellectual leaders of the Arab world to look with favor upon the totalitarian Powers after these had become the declared enemies of the Western nations.

Neither the Fascists nor the Nazis, once the Axis had been established, were slow to seize the advantages with which they were presented. German and Italian missionary schools throughout the Near East, and even in Palestine, became exceedingly active centers of propaganda. Axis consulates and commercial agencies were busy in spreading false reports, in arousing suspicions, and in reawakening old grievances in every Arab country.

As Eliahu Ben-Horin has explained in his admirable book *The Middle East,* no stranger paradox can be found in modern history than that to be found in the fact that Nazi penetration of the Near East during the critical years immediately before the Second World War was more greatly facilitated by the Jews than by their mortal enemies themselves.

Hitler's first anti-Semitic decrees caused the flight from Germany of all of those Jews who could readily abandon their homes. Soon, however, the form of persecution became far more drastic. Within a few months no Jews seeking to emigrate were permitted to take with them either money or valuables. These were confiscated. The only exception made was in the case of Jews who gave proof that they were bound for Palestine. The Nazi Government permitted German Jews emigrating to the Holy Land to take with them such funds as they could show had been derived from the sale within Palestine of goods exported from Germany.

In order to help rescue as many German Jews as possible, the Zionist financial institutions in Palestine actually entered into a transfer agreement with the German Reichsbank. Supervising agencies were established in Berlin and Tel Aviv. After this arrangement had been functioning for some time Doctor Schacht, then President of the Reichsbank, broadened the scope of the agreement so that it applied to all of the Near Eastern states, and not merely to Palestine. Jewish immigration into Palestine increased very rapidly. The foreign exchange accruing to the German Government as a result of these arrangements was correspondingly augmented. The leaders of the German-Jewish communities even agreed that high bonuses should be paid to all of the Near Eastern importers of German goods. Since these transactions undoubtedly save the lives of many thousands of German Jews they should not now be questioned. But it cannot be denied that they had greatly strengthened the political and economic influence of the Nazis in the Near East, particularly in North Africa and in the Levant, when the war came.

An embarrassing difficulty that Hitler faced in the Near East, once the war broke out, was how to reconcile in the Arab mind his claim that the slaughter of the Jews was due to their racial inferiority with his alleged admiration for the racial superiority of the Jews' fellow Semites, the Arabs.

When the British Government kept insisting upon the contradiction between slaughtering the Jews on the pretext that they were non-Aryan and proclaiming simultaneously that the equally Semitic Arabs were members of a superior race, the German Foreign Office could only angrily retort: "We have never said that the Arabs were inferior as a race. On the contrary, we have always pointed out the glorious past of the Arab people."

But such inconsistencies had little lasting result upon Arab thinking. Axis propaganda in the press was highly effective. The Arab-language programs that the Fascist Government broadcast from its radio station at Bari were even more successful. But it was, of course, the sweeping victories of the German blitzkrieg that were primarily responsible for transforming the latent sympathy of the Arabs for the Axis into overt support.

Although Egypt under the terms of her treaty with Great Britain was compelled to serve as the latter's principal military and naval base in the Mediterranean, the Egyptian Government had proclaimed its neutrality. Axis agents infested Cairo and Alexandria. The Court and the Departments of the Government were filled with Axis sympathizers. On several occasions the British authorities were obliged to resort to forceful measures in order to persuade the Egyptian Government to correct conditions which directly endangered Allied security. Had it not been for Britain's military strength in Egypt the outcome might well have been far different. As it was, when the victorious Rommel was advancing toward Alexandria, and had not yet been halted at El Alamein, a popular uprising in Cairo in support of the Axis was only averted by the narrowest of margins.

In Palestine, the Grand Mufti, Haj Amin el Husseini, who owed his appointment to a British High Commissioner, had long been an agent of the Nazi Government. He had been the instigator and the director of the Arab rebellion of 1936 against the British Administration. The

Mufti had won over a considerable number of young Arab nationalists to the Axis side. These, throughout the war, operated as an active fifth column in Palestine. The Mufti himself escaped to Italy. Until the war's close he flitted between Rome and Berlin seeking to help the Axis armies to gain control of the Near East.

The month of April, 1941, marked what was later seen to be the most critical period of the war. It seemed only barely possible that Great Britain, then fighting alone, could long hold out. Greece had at last been occupied. Rommel's capture of Alexandria seemed to be imminent. The Mufti's henchman, Rashid Ali Gailani, chose this moment to launch a revolt in Iraq. It came within an ace of succeeding. Had the small British force available not been able to crush the revolt before it had gathered momentum, the key Arab state of Iraq would have fallen into Nazi hands. For the main British armies in North Africa were so hard-pressed that they could have sent no re-enforcements to oppose the German air-borne forces that were poised in Greece and in Crete, ready to descend upon Iraq as soon as their native adherents had overthrown the Government and seized the airfields. With the German occupation of Iraq, the door would have been open for the Nazis to enter the Levant and Arabia. Since the United States was not yet a belligerent, the Japanese Navy could readily have joined the Germans and the Italians at the Suez Canal. The outcome of the war might well have been altogether different.

During these dark years when the fate of the Western countries hung in the balance the one element in all of the Near East that remained unalterably loyal to the cause of democracy was the Jewish community in Palestine.

Throughout the war the Palestine Jews besought the British for permission to form a Jewish army to fight at the side of the Allies. These offers were consistently rejected. The Jews were permitted to serve as technicians, in commissariats, and in labor battalions. But the British authorities adhered rigidly to a policy which only permitted the acceptance for combat service of a number of Jews equal to the number of Arab volunteers. Since the number of Arabs who volunteered was negligible, only a handful of Jews were permitted to join up. The hope of the younger Jews of Palestine that a Jewish army, with its own flag and insignia, would be allowed to fight in a war upon whose outcome their own fate depended was consequently never realized.

The most tragic aspect of the situation in Palestine during the war, however, was that which involved the refugees. It was the refugee problem more than any other question which helped to bring on the Palestine crisis that we now face.

As the war progressed, and as Hitler's mass liquidation of the Jews increased in scale and in horror, numberless thousands of men, women and children sought to flee for their lives from the countries of Central and Eastern Europe, as these regions fell one by one into Nazi hands. The problem of where those who survived might find shelter became paramount. Until her defeat no country in Western Europe had showed a greater measure of humanity in opening her doors to these refugees than France. But the number of those who could reach France, Great Britain, or the New World was infinitesimal compared to the number of those who found no road open to the West. When Hitler had occupied all of Western Europe there was left no avenue of escape save that to the East. The refugees streamed down through the Balkans like hunted animals. They sought frantically to find some chance to reach Palestine, or even Iran and East Africa.

The prohibition which the infamous White Paper of 1939 placed upon immigration into Palestine resulted in a needless sacrifice of uncounted lives. Even before the war broke out, ships were difficult to charter. The unseaworthy and rotten hulks, which were usually the only vessels that could be secured to transport refugees from ports in Southeastern Europe, not infrequently capsized. If they remained afloat they were readily overhauled by the British warships patrolling the Eastern Mediterranean which then turned them away from the shores of Palestine.

The stream of illegal immigration into Palestine had commenced in 1936. By 1939 it had become a flood. Until the war broke out, the British Government brought constant pressure to bear upon the Rumanian, Yugoslav, and Greek Governments to forbid the departure of refugee ships from their ports. The ships that did succeed in putting out from the Rumanian ports of Constanza and Galati, and that were able to pass through the naval patrol, were forbidden by the British military authorities in Palestine to land their human cargoes. Refugee ships were even fired upon from shore batteries. But the indignation of the British House of Commons was fortunately so strong when it learned of this cold-blooded insistence upon depriving these tragic wanderers of their one chance for survival, that the practice was abandoned. Eventually those refugees who arrived in Palestine illegally were placed in concentration camps for the duration of the war, while punitive fines were exacted from the owners and officers of the vessels upon which they had shipped.

Occasionally groups of refugees went to Constantinople in the hope that permission might there be given them to travel overland to Palestine. In such cases, however, their chances were virtually nil. For not only was the British Government firm in its refusal to make exceptions, but the opposition of the authorities in the Arab states through which they would have to pass in order to reach Palestine was adamant.

In the spring of 1941 I received word in the Department of State that five hundred Jewish children, most of them orphans or without known relatives, had been collected in Rumania and had from there been sent to Constantinople. As a rare exception the British Government had granted them temporary asylum in Palestine. They could travel safely by way of Iraq. Only Turkish authorities were willing to afford every facility. Only a transit permit from the Iraqi Government was needed. Notwithstanding the appeals made by the United States Government directly to Nuri Pasha, then Prime Minister of Iraq, and an Arab statesman highly regarded for his Western outlook, the Government which he headed stubbornly refused to grant these children the right to reach their haven of safety.

Soon after Hitler began his campaign against the Jews, and when all official remonstrances had proved to be futile, President Roosevelt tried to find some way to hasten the emigration of the Jews from Central Europe. What to him was equally important was to discover a safe refuge for them in some other part of the world.

Granted the policy then being pursued by the Chamberlain Cabinet, Palestine could offer a refuge to only a few thousand. The President, at first through personal correspondence with the Presidents of other American Republics, attempted to negotiate an agreement upon some co-ordinated plan by which the more sparsely settled countries of South America, such as Brazil, Venezuela and Colombia, would open their doors each year to a fixed number of refugee families and provide these immigrants with the land and financial assistance they needed until they could become self-supporting.

It was soon evident, however, that the problem had become so vast that no program such as this could meet the constantly growing requirements of what might well become a mass migration.

President Roosevelt, consequently, summoned an International Conference on Refugees. It was attended by representatives of all but the Axis countries. The conference met in the autumn of 1938 at Evian. There an agreement was reached for the establishment of an intergovermental committee on refugees designed to set up the machinery needed to facilitate the emigration of European refugees, and at the same time, through negotiation with individual governments, to bring about the acceptance by all suitable countries of refugee families for permanent settlement.

This intergovernmental committee was intended to take over the functions of an agency of the League of Nations which had failed to achieve any practical results. Unfortunately, when the war broke out a year later, notwithstanding the valiant efforts of many of the officials of this new intergovernmental committee, the organization was faced with insuperable obstacles. It had little chance to relieve the plight of the refugees.

For reasons of security, immigration restrictions in all countries grew far more rigorous after the war broke out. The financial burdens that the resettlement of refugees involved were now too heavy for governments confronting the requirements for all-out defense. The hopes of the leaders of the Jewish communities in the New World, as well as in Europe, consequently became centered upon Palestine as the only solution for the problems resulting from the catastrophe which had overwhelmed their people.

And, as the war drew to a close, the Jewish survivors in Europe, whether they were lingering on in concentration camps, in exile in Siberia, or hiding here and there as best they might in the countries still occupied by the Axis, turned their eyes toward Palestine as their one hope of ever gaining a home, security, and the opportunity to lead a new and happier life.

That hope had been strengthened by the statement made by President Roosevelt on March 16, 1944:

> The American Government has never given its approval to the White Paper of 1939. The President is happy that the doors of Palestine are open today to Jewish refugees and that when future decisions are reached, full justice will be done to those who seek a Jewish National Home, for which our Government and the American people have always had the deepest sympathy, and today more than ever, in view of the tragic plight of hundreds of thousands of homeless Jewish refugees.

It is not surprising that Zionism, rapidly as it had grown during the years before the war, should have represented a dynamic force at the war's end.

What may seem at first glance to be unaccountable is that the day of victory should have brought no modification of the policy of the British Government. Yet the reasons are not hard to find.

By the summer of 1945 the British people began to realize that Britain had exhausted herself in her struggle against the Axis, and that the victory of the United Nations could not spell that end of restrictions, of privation and of unceasing toil for which they had hoped.

Whether or not Winston Churchill would preside over it, the liquidation of a major part of the British Empire had become inevitable.

As this realization of the hard truth sank in, it was only natural that British public opinion should, at least at first, have insisted that if Britain was to continue to be a great power some means must be found to salvage her preponderant position in the Near East, in order to retain assured access to her oil resources and to safeguard her position in Africa.

The war had emphasized the strategic value of Palestine as the key to the Eastern Mediterranean, as a base which affords air and naval supremacy in the areas adjacent to the Suez Canal and in the Red Sea, as by far the safest and cheapest outlet for the Arabian oil fields, and as the only possible alternative bastion for Great Britain's naval and military forces when these had to be withdrawn from Egypt.

It was equally evident that in the event, then as yet only dimly forecast, that the Soviet Union should seek to dominate the Dardanelles, the Balkan Peninsula, and the Eastern Mediterranean, the retention of Palestine in British hands could prove to be of determining, strategic importance.

It was for these reasons that the new Labor Cabinet's policy toward Palestine seemed to be precisely the same as that developed under the Cabinet of Neville Chamberlain.

For the time being Mr. Attlee and his colleagues adopted a policy of procrastination in the hope that "something might turn up."

3

Attempts to Find a Palestine Solution

Except for Woodrow Wilson, no President of the United States has shown greater sympathy for Zionism than Franklin Roosevelt. He was also determined to find some rapid means of helping the European Jews who wished to emigrate. It had been his expectation, as I have shown, that a solution might be found by the Intergovernmental Committee on Refugees. When that agency was stalemated by the war, President Roosevelt gave increased thought to Palestine as a haven for immediate resettlement.

The President hoped throughout the war that a just and practical settlement of the Palestine controversy could still be found by direct negotiations between Jewish and Arab leaders. He was, of course, fully advised of the repeated attempts to negotiate that had been made under the direction of Doctor Chaim Weizmann. He was by no means convinced that the failure of these efforts necessarily implied the existence of any insuperable obstacle. He regarded the agreement reached after the First World War between Doctor Weizmann and the Emir Feisal, the most enlightened Arab statesman of modern times, as an encouraging precedent.

Both prior to 1939, as well as after the war had broken out, the President conferred repeatedly at the White House with Zionist leaders. At many of these conferences I myself was present. He developed in these meetings the arguments that he felt should be advanced in behalf of the establishment of a Jewish Commonwealth. He unequivocally supported the assurances given in the Balfour Declaration. He believed that the creation of the promised Homeland would not only afford security and an assured future for many hundreds of thousands of Jews who would otherwise be homeless, but that such a Commonwealth would also provide a most valuable demonstration to the peoples of the Near East of an advanced form of democratic state, and that the example given and the influence exercised by such a state would be bound within a relatively short time to raise living standards in the adjacent countries.

President Roosevelt was deeply interested in the possibilities for industrial and agricultural development within Palestine. I have heard him assert upon several occasions that it was his hope that once a Palestine Commonwealth had been successfully established, the neighboring states of Syria, the Lebanon, and Trans-Jordan would be persuaded of the advantages they would secure by a federal union with Palestine, within which customs and currency barriers could gradually be eliminated, and under which far-reaching projects for irrigation, power development, and the construction of communications might be carried out by common agreement. He thought the economic benefits the Arab countries would obtain, particularly through increased foreign investment, and the development of natural resources, would be an inducement to the Arab leaders and their peoples sufficient to overcome racial antagonism. The President was a firm believer in the appeal of reason and of self-interest. He underestimated in this case the strength of Arab nationalism.

The President, however, saw quite realistically that the best time to settle the Palestine question permanently would be when the peace settlements were negotiated. He said to me on one occasion that if, upon the defeat of the Axis, direct negotiations still proved fruitless, the United Nations organization to be set up after the war would then have to undertake the creation of a Commonwealth of Palestine, and protect this new state by an international police force until it could protect itself. But President Roosevelt always hoped that a settlement could be negotiated by representative leaders of the Jewish people and representative leaders of the Arabs, and that no solution need be imposed.

There has been much malicious misrepresentation of what took place when the King of Saudi Arabia conferred with the President in Alexandria while the latter was on his way home from the Yalta Conference.

I am confident that the President in his conference with King Ibn Saud did not modify in one iota the basic principles that he had consistently supported. He hoped for a negotiated settlement of the Palestine question. But the kind of settlement he envisaged was one that would provide the Jews with their promised national homeland. The official letters, sent to King Ibn Saud after the President had returned to Washington, were prepared by the Department of State for the President's signature during those last weeks of the President's life when he was unable to devote much time or thought to official correspondence. Even so, open to misinterpretation as some of the phrases used may seem to be, there is in those letters no commitment which is at variance with the views which the President had previously maintained.

Mr. Churchill was replaced as Prime Minister only a few months after the death of President Roosevelt. The two outstanding supporters of Jewish aspirations in Palestine were thus removed from authority at the very time when their influence would have proved decisive.

Mr. Churchill had been a member of the Lloyd George Cabinet that had issued the Balfour Declaration. He had consistently upheld many of the objectives of the Zionists. When the Chamberlain Cabinet, in 1937, ignored the recommendations of the Peel Commission, Mr. Churchill had vigorously assailed the failure of the British Government to envisage any constructive remedy for a situation that was steadily deteriorating, and had stoutly maintained that the courses of repudiation, of drift and of indecision that the British Government was pursuing could only end in disaster.

When Mr. Churchill came to the United States in 1946 for a much needed rest, he told me of his deep interest in Palestine, and of the part which he had played in earlier years in supporting the right of the Jews to the fulfillment of the pledges given them in the Balfour Declaration. We had been speaking of the appalling difficulties which the British Government was at that moment facing in India. I had ventured the opinion that no settlement of the Indian question would be found unless the demand of the Moslems for an independent Pakistan was granted, and I had added that my thinking had been greatly influenced by the conviction to which I had slowly and reluctantly come, that in the case of Palestine only some form of partition could now solve what would otherwise remain an insoluble problem. Mr. Churchill was gratified, and apparently surprised, by what I told him. He said that in both of these cases the accumulated errors of the past now made necessary solutions that were far from perfect, but which at least contained the essential basis of justice, and offered the best chance of avoiding far greater difficulties in the future. His chief emphasis was laid upon the need for prompt and decisive action.

The British Labor Party had consistently upheld the Zionist cause. In its party platforms it had attacked the Palestine policies of the Baldwin and Chamberlain Cabinets as bitterly as Mr. Churchill himself. When Mr. Attlee succeeded Mr. Churchill as Prime Minister, it was assumed that the new Government would rapidly undertake a policy which would give the Jewish people their long-awaited independent commonwealth. Unfortunately the contrary proved to be the case.

There were many Labor members in the new House of Commons, and several Ministers in the Attlee Cabinet, who favored the termination of the British mandate, the establishment under British auspices of a free Palestine, and an open door in the Holy Land to the Jewish refugees of Europe. But their views, strongly as they were voiced, were disregarded. This was due to the persistent opposition of Mr. Bevin, the new Secretary of State for Foreign Affairs, and to the traditional recalcitrance of the permanent officials of the British Foreign and Colonial Offices. British policy in Palestine remained to all intents and purposes the same as that followed by the Chamberlain Cabinet.

The tragedy of the Jewish refugees confined in the Central European concentration camps for displaced persons had become so desperate by the late summer of 1945 that public opinion in the United States began to make itself heard. President Truman was informed by his political advisers that Governor Dewey of New York was about to offer publicly some plan for their relief.

The President at once issued a statement to the press that he was urging the British Government to permit one hundred thousand destitute Jewish refugees to be transported from Europe to Palestine. No indication was, however, given that the Government of the United States had any idea either of meeting the heavy costs which this resettlement would involve, or of helping to protect the Jews in Palestine from the Arab retaliation which this new large-scale immigration would provoke.

At a moment when Britain was feeling the first impact of the financial and economic crisis caused by her war effort, this appeal from the President of the United States, of which she had had no prior warning, was hardly likely to produce beneficial results. In fact all that it produced was extreme irritation on the part of the British public, and an official announcement from the British Government that it would consider the appeal when the United States expressed some inclination to assume the obligations that it would involve.

Nor was it long before the Jews of Palestine, the sufferers in the European concentration camps, and many of the Jewish leaders in the United States, were forced to the conclusion that this appeal, and similar appeals which the President later directed to the British Government, had been made primarily for political reasons. There continued to be no sign that the American Government intended to assume any direct responsibility in the measures needed to relieve the conditions of which it complained.

Finally, when the Administration in Washington realized that public opinion could no longer be deluded into thinking that mere words of sympathy for the refugees constituted an adequate contribution on the part of the United States to a solution of the Palestine problem, a new experiment was made. From the standpoint of the Administration this new approach possessed the great advantage of demonstrating continued sympathy for the Jews while involving the American Government in no material responsibilities.

A group of American officials, headed by Henry F. Grady, was sent to London to "explore" with members of the British Government the possibility of elaborating a Palestine settlement. Out of these conferences eventually emerged the so-called Morrison-Grady plan. Largely drafted by the permanent officials of the British Colonial Office, the plan provided for the permanent domination by Britain of Palestine, Arab occupation of most of the territory, and the relegation of the Jews to what has been aptly termed a "ghetto." The storm of protests aroused when this fantastic "settlement" was prematurely published, caused consternation in the White House. Mr. Gray – a most able public servant, but unfortunately wholly unprepared for the task entrusted to him – was publicly disavowed.

It was obvious that some new experiment must be quickly launched if the Administration was not to suffer serious political prejudice from the Morrison-Grady fiasco.

Announcement was therefore made on December 10, 1945, that the American and British Governments had decided to establish an Anglo-American Committee of Inquiry on Palestine and on the conditions of the Jews in Europe. The announcement stated that the Committee had been created:

> (1) To examine political, economic and social conditions in Palestine as they bear upon the problem of Jewish immigration and settlement therein and the well-being of the peoples now living therein.

(2) To examine the position of the Jews in those countries in Europe where they have been the victims of Nazi and Fascist persecution, and the practical measures taken or contemplated to be taken in those countries to enable them to live free from discrimination and oppression and to make estimates of those who wish or will be impelled by their conditions to migrate to Palestine or other countries outside Europe.

(3) To hear the views of competent witnesses and to consult representative Arabs and Jews on the problems of Palestine as such problems are affected by conditions subject to examination under paragraphs (1) and (2) above and by other relevant facts and circumstances; and to make recommendations to the Governments of the United States and of the United Kingdom for an interim handling of those problems as well as for their permanent solution; and

(4) To make such other recommendations to the Governments of the United States and of the United Kingdom as may be necessary to meet the immediate needs arising from conditions subject to examination under paragraph (2) above by remedial action in the European countries in question, or by the provision of facilities for immigration to and settlement in countries outside Europe.

The Committee was to be composed of six Americans and six British members, and its report was to be rendered within four months.

The inherent defect in the appointment of such a committee was patent. There had been no dearth of official commissions appointed to investigate conditions in Palestine and to recommend solutions for the problem. Not one of their reports had ever yet been productive of beneficial results. Now that the League of Nations no longer existed, Great Britain had assumed sole authority in Palestine. Only if the British Government had given a prior commitment that it would either obligate itself to carry out the recommendations that this new committee might make, or at least regard them as the basis for a new policy, could the establishment of the Committee have had any justification.

For the moment was desperately urgent. The condition of the homeless and destitute Jews of Europe, confined in their concentration camps under British or American supervision, was becoming increasingly hopeless. The news that they were now to have no prospect of any change in their status for at least four months, while the Committee was carrying on its investigation and preparing its report, came to them as a new blow. Few Jews had any confidence that the appointment of a committee was more than a mere effort to stall for time. The feeling was general that it represented an attempt on the part of the British Government to postpone the day when remedial action would have to be taken in Palestine, and an all too obvious attempt on the part of the Administration in Washington to play politics with an issue which directly involved the fate of great numbers of suffering people.

The Anglo-American Committee conducted hearings in the United States and in Great Britain. It traveled through the countries of Central Europe and heard many of the "displaced persons." It visited Palestine, made a thorough survey of conditions there, and arranged for comprehensive hearings in the Holy Land. The American members, and a majority of the British members, were enlightened and humane men, inspired with a sincere desire to hasten the just settlement of a problem that was becoming increasingly grave as the days passed.

The Committee's Report was published in the spring of 1946. It was met with an outburst of violent recrimination throughout the Arab states, and with bitter disappointment on the part of the Jews.

The Report recommended that one hundred thousand

Jewish refugees be admitted immediately into Palestine, and it urged the need for many reforms in the administration of the country, particularly in connection with the problem of land tenure. But the Committee recommended that Palestine should not become a Jewish Commonwealth. One American member and one British member strongly believed in partition with the creation of two independent states, one Jewish and one Arab. Because, however, of their thought that a unanimous report would have a better chance of being implemented by the British Government, they joined in signing the recommendation of the majority. The Committee further proposed that an international trusteeship over Palestine be eventually established under the United Nations, and, by implication, indicated its belief that the administering Power, under the United Nations, should continue to be Great Britain.

President Truman endorsed that part of the Report which recommended the admission of one hundred thousand refugees into Palestine. He withheld comment upon the further recommendations. The British Government declared that American military and financial assistance would be required if the Committee's recommendations were to be carried out. Both the British and American Governments announced that further consultation with Arab and Jewish leaders would be necessary before any action could be taken. As had been anticipated by many, the work of the Committee had gone for nothing. The situation remained precisely as it had been before the Committee's appointment.

It should not be overlooked that the British Foreign Secretary, Mr. Bevin, had told several members of the Committee, when they were in London during the course of their investigations, that the British Government would adopt the Committee's findings. "We shall accept your recommendations," he categorically declared.

Mr. Bartley Crum, outstanding among the American members of the Committee for his passionate faith in the justice of the Zionist cause, and one who has long most eloquently urged that the establishment of a free and democratic Jewish state in the Near East would provide a rampart for Western democracy and a guarantee for the future security of the United States, has made this comment in his book *Behind the Silken Curtain*:

> The fate of our Committee's recommendation is one of the scandals of this post-war period. There is absolutely no question that every American member of the Committee — and I think the British members — believed that, as Mr. Ernest Bevin had promised, our recommendations would be carried out. I find it painful to admit that Dr. Albert Einstein, Dr. Abba Hillel Silver, the American Zionist leader, and others who characterized the Committee's appointment as a device to postpone action, were correct.

The months of 1946 dragged on. The recommendations of the Anglo-American Committee were soon forgotten.

As a major concession the British Government was permitting fifteen hundred Jews to enter Palestine each month; and this at a time when hundreds of thousands of homeless Jews were rotting morally and physically in their prison barracks, unable to return to their homes, and seeking desperately some means of reaching Palestine.

Illegal immigration constantly increased. Shiploads of refugees were continually intercepted by the British Navy. They were then removed to Cyprus there to be incarcerated in new prison camps. Acts of violence against the British authorities in Palestine rapidly mounted. The attempt of the British military administration to put down what had already become an uprising of a people determined to be free, resulted in the arrest of two thousand Jewish leaders, the execution of not a few young extremists, and the temporary abolition of the rights and prerogatives of the Jewish Agency.

There could be little question of the justice of Doctor Chaim Weizmann's characterization of these measures as an "assault by the mandatory government on the Jewish people of Palestine."

In an effort to stem the tide of criticism now rising throughout the United States, and evident as well in Great Britain, Mr. Bevin once more resorted to the shopworn plan of summoning Jewish and Arab leaders to round-table conferences in London. This device soon proved to be as futile as it had been in the past. The Arab League refused to participate. While representatives of the Jewish Agency once more expressed their willingness to employ every means within their power to bring about a negotiated settlement, they made no attempt to conceal their conviction that the time had long since passed when such measures could be productive of any possible benefit.

Nor was public opinion in the United States mollified by a singularly intemperate and cruelly unjust reflection upon the Jews of New York which Mr. Bevin voiced in a public address at Bournemouth in the autumn of 1946.

In the meantime the world horizon was rapidly darkening. Tension between the Soviet Union and the Western Powers was increasing. To the far-sighted it was already apparent that the Near East was in danger of becoming the scene of a prolonged contest between the Soviet Union and the Western democracies. It was clear that the failure to find a prompt settlement of the Palestine dispute would increase the likelihood of an outbreak of open hostilities in the Eastern Mediterranean. And were the British, the Jews, and the Arabs to be involved in such hostilities, there would be scant probability that the area or scope of such a conflict could be restricted, or that these hostilities would not eventually draw in the remaining major Powers and prove to be the cause of the dreaded Third World War.

The prolonged refusal of the British Government to consider any solution that might have weakened its hold on Palestine was partly due to the British General Staff, who hoped that after the withdrawal of Britain's forces from Egypt, Palestine could become her strategic base in the Near East. The Port of Haifa had already been enlarged as a major naval base. The construction in Southern Palestine of British air bases was being rushed. The number of British troops concentrated in Palestine amounted to at least one hundred thousand men. Yet the financial straits in which Great Britain found herself, the increasing unwillingness of the British people to view with equanimity the drain upon their diminishing resources represented by the establishment of a vast British military base in Palestine, and the increasing number of British lives that were being lost in putting down Jewish resistance, were all factors which forced the Government at length to realize that it could no longer proceed with its initial plans.

Winston Churchill, in the House of Commons, was the spokesman for a wide sector of public opinion that condemned the Government's policy in Palestine, and that demanded an immediate withdrawal by Great Britain from the responsibilities that she had undertaken under her mandate.

Simultaneously, many here in the United States had come to the conclusion that the problem of Palestine was no longer a question that could be solved by a British

Government, with or without the platonic support of the United States. It had clearly become a challenge that must be met by the United Nations.

I expressed this belief early in 1946:

> The Commonwealth will come into being only when the United Nations decides, as it must, that the establishment of a Jewish Commonwealth in Palestine is essential to world peace and to world stability. Unless . . . the United Nations is charged with the obligation of carrying out such a decision the Commonwealth of Palestine will continue to be an ideal and not a reality. Only the United Nations itself, representing the concerted determination of the free peoples of the world, will possess the necessary authority to achieve a final solution of the Palestine problem.

Later in the same year I wrote these words:

> Should the United Nations take such action as that urged in the preceding paragraphs, the Arab states would be unable to oppose it. . . . The forces that the United Nations might have to send to Palestine to preserve order during the first stages of an independent Commonwealth need be very small indeed. . . .
>
> The United States . . . should immediately assume leadership within the United Nations in having the organization accept the responsibility for finding a permanent and just solution of the Palestine issues. That opportunity will now be presented at the meeting of the General Assembly in the autumn of 1946. For unless all of the major powers share in that responsibility, Palestine may well become the spark which will light a vast conflagration.

The opportunity afforded the Government of the United States to take such an initiative while there was still time to avert many of the dangers which have since arisen, was not seized. All that was heard from the White House were further empty phrases of sympathy for the Jewish people, and continued expressions of pious hope that the British would permit the immediate entrance of one hundred thousand refugees into a Palestine that was already devastated by violence, and where there was security for neither life nor property.

When the pressure of public opinion had finally become too great to make further resistance possible, and only after many British, Jewish, and Arab lives had been needlessly sacrificed, the British Government bowed to the inevitable.

On February 14, 1947, the Government of the United Kingdom officially declared that it had failed to find any solution for the problem of Palestine. It announced that it would request the United Nations to recommend a solution.

4

The United Nations and Palestine

On April 2, 1947, in a letter to the Secretary General of the United Nations, the British Government asked that the question of Palestine be placed upon the agenda for the next regular session of the General Assembly, so that the Assembly might make recommendations as to the future government of Palestine. It further requested that a special session of the Assembly be summoned to appoint a committee to prepare the basis for these recommendations.

The authority of the Assembly to take the action asked by Great Britain is provided by Article 10 of the United Nations Charter. This Article reads as follows:

> The General Assembly may discuss any question or any matters within the scope of the present Charter or relating to the powers and functions of any organs provided for in the present Charter and . . . may make recommendations to the members of the United Nations or to the Security Council or to both on any such questions or matters.

From the time when the British Government submitted the Palestine question to the United Nations, concerted efforts have been made, with no little success, to convince public opinion in the United States and in the other democracies that the United Nations possesses no inherent authority over Palestine and that its intervention for the purpose of deciding upon whatever solution seems to it most equitable, and best calculated to be lasting, is only warranted to the extent of an advisory opinion as requested by the British Government.

These attempts have to no small extent been inspired by those powerful forces that oppose the creation of an independent Jewish Commonwealth. While the various groups and interests of which these forces are composed are wholly unrelated, they have nevertheless been cooperating closely in their common cause.

The first is represented by the propagandists for the Arab Higher Committee of Palestine and by the executive agency of the federation of the Arab states, known as the Arab League. These deny that any Power, whether the United Nations or an individual nation, has the authority to question the right of the Arabs of Palestine to exercise sole jurisdiction over that entire region. Because the Palestinian Arabs represent a considerable majority of the population of the Holy Land, these propagandists maintain that under the principle of self-determination the Jewish minority possesses no right to have any voice in deciding what the future status of that country shall be. They refuse to recognize as valid the pledges contained in the Balfour Declaration, the ratification of those pledges officially given by all of the Allied Governments after the First World War, or the incorporation by the League of Nations of those pledges in the mandate over Palestine which the League conferred upon Great Britain. They ignore as of no weight the fact that the Arabs of Palestine have not been an independent nation, that Turkey exercised sovereignty in Palestine, that Turkey by treaty ceded Palestine to the Allies by whom she had been conquered, and that the Allies in turn vested sovereignty over Palestine in the League of Nations. On the sole ground that the Arabs constitute a majority of Palestine's population and have inhabited the country for many centuries, they insistently maintain that the United Nations has no vestige of right to recommend or impose any solution for the problem of Palestine, unless that solution is one that meets with Arab approval.

Among the other groups that are bent upon preventing any action by the United Nations which might recognize as legitimate the rights asserted by the Jewish people, are to be found that very substantial body of opinion in Great Britain which holds that British hegemony in the Arab world is essential if the British Empire is to be preserved, and that any solution which antagonized the Arabs would be counter to British interests; the politically potent British and American oil companies which have received concessions in the Arab countries, and which allege that the success of the Zionist cause would jeopardize their own interests, which they of course identify with the national interests of the Western democracies; the fanatical Jew-haters in Western Europe and in the United States who devote themselves to the spread of anti-Semitism by any and every means available to them, and whose recent pleas for the "poor Arabs" have been peculiarly unconvincing; and a number of wholly honorable Americans obsessed with the fear that should the United Nations attempt to formulate, much more to enforce, any decision with regard to Palestine that might run into armed opposition, it would involve the United States in war.

Finally there are two far more influential bodies of opinion, which, while not denying the authority of the United Nations to make recommendations as to a future government of Palestine, are totally opposed to any action by the United Nations that might result in the establishment of a Jewish Commonwealth.

The first of these is represented by those Jews who are opposed to Zionism and who strongly deprecate any attempt to reconstitute a Jewish nation.

The second, by those authorities, both in as well as out of Government, who believe that the Charter of the United Nations does not empower the Security Council to use force to implement a political settlement, such as the plan for the partition of Palestine, whether recommended by the General Assembly or by the Security Council itself.

The fallacies in the claims of the Arab propagandists have already been exposed. What I believe to be the basic error involved in the position of those who would restrict the powers of the Security Council will be dealt with subsequently.

It is desirable at this point to answer the question raised by those who oppose action on the Palestine problem by the United Nations on the ground that the authority over Palestine formerly held by the League of Nations is not necessarily vested in the United Nations, and whose views, strangely enough, have only very recently been re-enforced by the position taken by the United States.

The official view of the American Government, as given by Ambassador Austin to the delegates at the special session of the Assembly of April, 1948, which was at variance with the view earlier expressed, and which, judging from the history of the preceding five months, might at any time be modified or even totally reversed, would seem to be as follows:

Sovereign jurisdiction over Palestine was vested in the League of Nations by the victorious Allies of the First World War who signed the Treaty of Sèvres with Turkey.

The League then conferred the Palestine mandate on Great Britain. Britain is now relinquishing her mandate. Since the League no longer exists, the authority to decide the fate of Palestine must consequently revert to what the American Government terms "the remaining members" of the Allies of the First World War, namely Great Britain, France and the United States.

As a specious argument, this would be hard to equal. The reason for it – to exclude the Soviet Union from any participation in the decision on Palestine – was obvious. But apart from its purely legalistic aspects, the inherent fallacy is plain.

Largely because of the unswerving persistence of Woodrow Wilson, the Covenant of the League of Nations provided in Article 22 for the mandate, or trusteeship, system, so that the rights of peoples who had not yet secured independence would be respected. It was for that reason that when Great Britain wished to secure control over Palestine she was unable to obtain sovereign rights, but only the rights of a mandatory Power. Supreme authority was vested in the League of Nations as the representative of the organized community of nations. It is true that the League of Nations as such is dead. But the organized community of nations has been revived as the United Nations.

If the April 1948 view of the American Government were to prevail, it would mean that three great Powers acting alone, rather than the family of nations, could decide the future of the peoples of Palestine. We would be returning to the days when great Powers decided the fate of peoples as though they were cattle. We would also be violating the spirit, and the clear intent, of the Charter of the United Nations.

Chapter XII of the Charter contains provisions specifying the method by which nations holding mandates from the League of Nations for "the administration of territories whose peoples have not yet attained a full measure of self-government" may, "by individual agreements," place these territories under the International Trusteeship system created by that Charter. It is true that Great Britain has not concluded any such agreement with respect to Palestine.

But Article 85 of the Charter stipulates that "the functions of the United Nations with regard to trusteeship agreements for all areas not designated as strategic, including the approval of the terms of the trusteeship agreements and of their alteration or amendment, shall be exercised by the General Assembly."

Great Britain officially notified the United Nations of her decision to terminate her mandate for Palestine and announced that she would relinquish all of the obligations assumed under that mandate on May 15, 1948. Under the terms of Article 85, above quoted, the General Assembly of the United Nations upon that date consequently became the sole authority capable of determining the fate of Palestine. The Assembly might or might not call upon the Trusteeship Council to assume control of the administration of Palestine after Britain's withdrawal. It had equal power and right to deal with Palestine through a special agency, such as that established to carry out the partition plan first recommended by the Assembly at its session of November, 1947, or to take such other action as it might deem best. It speaks for the organized moral opinion of all peoples.

The justification for the Jewish claims to Palestine, the lack of foundation for the Arab demand for exclusive jurisdiction, the authority possessed by the United Nations, and the nature of the forces that oppose the establishment of an independent Jewish Commonwealth have now been explored.

There is perhaps a higher justification for holding that the United Nations must settle the Palestine problem than that to be found in any merely legal or technical considerations.

During the thirty years that have passed since the issuance of the Balfour Declaration, the Jews in Palestine have become a community of more than six hundred thousand souls. They have brought enlightenment and great material prosperity to the land where they have settled. Jewish communities throughout the world have spent many hundreds of millions of dollars within Palestine. The Jews have advanced rapidly toward the creation of a new nation. All this has been done because of their reliance upon the pledges given them by organized international society as set forth in the mandate established by the League of Nations.

The United Nations confronts these accomplished facts. Can they be lightly disregarded?

But the United Nations also faces another accomplished fact, and this, one of the most horrifying, and one of the most tragic, in recorded history.

Six millions of the Jews of Europe were slaughtered at Hitler's behest. The survivors are homeless and destitute. In their vast majority they do not wish to go back to the places of their origin. They cannot face the scenes where their families and their friends were taken away to torture and to death. They fear the poison of anti-Semitism that still infects the countries of their birth. They have no private means which would enable them to emigrate. Only a handful of countries in the Western world are as yet willing to open their doors to them. They still, three years after the end of the war, are confined like criminals in concentration camps. Only Palestine offers them a place of refuge and the hope for a new and better life.

This is the human challenge that the United Nations must meet as it deals with the Palestine question. How can the moral opinion of the world, represented in the United Nations, refuse to sanction the positive and decisive action needed to save these sorrowful refugees, unwanted as they are anywhere else in the world, and give them a chance to live under new skies, in dignity and safety? All of the Western nations, in greater or lesser degree, must share in the responsibility for those world conditions which permitted the rise of Hitlerism and the mass murders of the Jews of which it was guilty. Are they now willing to fail in accomplishing such atonement as is now still possible – that is, to secure through the United Nations a final settlement of the Palestine problem that will provide moral and physical rehabilitation for the hundreds of thousands of refugees who can find it in no other way?

Can it be seriously contended by an enlightened opinion in any part of the world that the United Nations can refuse to meet this humanitarian challenge, or refrain from recognizing the facts as they exist, and still maintain that it is carrying out the obligations with which it is charged? Are the feudal lords of Arabia to be permitted by the United Nations to insist successfully that that small area of Palestine allotted to the Jews under the partition plan shall now be refused to them and to the suffering members of their race in Europe, when the vast regions under the control of the Arabs are largely uninhabited, and as yet largely undeveloped?

Were the Arab pretensions to be sustained, and were the United Nations to refuse to assume the authority required to impose a Palestine solution that recognized the justice of the Jewish claims, and that met adequately and courageously the challenge offered by the continuing tragedy of the European refugees, what would then be the value of those great words set forth in the Preamble of the United Nations?

> To reaffirm faith in fundamental human rights, in the dignity and worth of the human person, in the equal rights of men and women and nations large and small:
>
> To establish conditions under which justice and respect for the obligations arising from treaties and other sources of international law can be maintained, and to promote social progress and better standards of life and larger freedom.

Many among those who have opposed, for one reason or another, all action by the United Nations that might satisfy the hopes of the Jewish people, have vehemently urged that further efforts be made, before the United Nations undertakes any more steps, to bring about some compromise settlement by direct negotiation between Jews and Arabs. These demands have also very recently been strongly re-enforced by the new official position of the United States.

The best reply that can be made is to be found in the words, which then represented the American position, and which were addressed to the Assembly of the United Nations in November, 1947, by Ambassador Herschel Johnson, a delegate of the United States:

> Much has been said . . . on the desirability and necessity of . . . a plan which would command the agreement of both the principle protagonists in this situation . . . No plan has ever been presented, either to this Assembly or to the mandatory government during its long years of ten-

> ure, or in any other place, which would meet with the acceptance of both the Arabs and the Jews. No such plan has ever been presented and I do not believe that any such plan will ever be presented. . . . Neither the Jews nor the Arabs will ever be completely satisfied with anything we do and it is just as well to bear that in mind.

Nor should it be forgotten that the partition plan adopted by the Assembly of the United Nations, when Mr. Johnson spoke, offered the Jews only the barest vestige of that for which they had hoped. What they were granted was rightly termed by the leaders of the Jewish Agency "an irreducible minimum." Were it to be still further diminished, they could neither create a viable state nor offer refuge to additional immigrants. Is it to be expected, even if Arab recalcitrance made it possible, that the Jews should enter new negotiations of which the only outcome must be a demand for further concessions on their part?

Here, then, is a problem of long standing which has grown more acute with the passage of the years, and which has been brought to a crisis by the crimes against humanity which Nazism perpetrated, and by the new tensions that have arisen since the Second World War. The British Government has announced that it is powerless to solve it, and that it is abandoning its responsibilities. If the crisis in Palestine remains unsolved, anarchy, chaos and increasing bloodshed will be the consequence. In the wake of the ensuing hostilities the conflicting interests in the Near East of the major Powers might well touch off a major conflagration from which a new world war would arise.

Can the United Nations conceivably refrain from asserting its obligations to take those remedial measures necessary to avert a new world calamity? Can such articles of the United Nations Charter as Articles 34 and 35 be disregarded? They read as follows:

> The Security Council may investigate any dispute or any situation which might lead to international friction or give rise to a dispute in order to determine whether the continuance of the dispute or situation is likely to endanger the maintenance of international peace and security.
>
> Any member of the United Nations may bring any dispute or any situation of the nature referred to in Article 34 to the attention of the Security Council or of the General Assembly.

To those who believe that the future of humanity depends upon the achievement of collective security as envisaged in the Charter of the United Nations, the imposition by the United Nations of a just and lasting solution of the Palestine problem has long since seemed an imperative necessity.

Lurking behind the problem of Palestine is to be found the whole bitter issue of anti-Semitism.

There are too many of us here in the United States who find it more agreeable to ignore this aspect of the problem and to blind ourselves to the shameful truth that it exists here in our own midst. Our country fought in the Second World War to bring about the creation of a world order of which the four freedoms were to be a cornerstone, and under which every man and woman would enjoy the right to live free from all discrimination in his homeland.

Some of us have found it hard to understand why it would not be wiser to fight this evil openly and insist that the Displaced Persons of Europe be assured by the United Nations of humane and non-discriminatory treatment in the countries where they were born. They see no valid reason for an exodus of refugees from Europe.

But few of these Americans have had any personal experience of the miasma of anti-Semitism which still hangs over Europe. Nor can they appreciate the depth of the longing of the European refugees for peace and for safety and for a place where they can be sure they "belong."

The attainment by the Jewish people of their long-awaited Promised Land is not the whole answer to the curse of anti-Semitism. Anti-Semitism cannot be eradicated until the hearts and minds of men and women in many parts of the world have undergone a drastic change, and until the democratic peoples themselves see that those declarations of faith in human liberty of which they boast can no longer continue to be mere empty phrases if the world of the future is to become truly free.

But the establishment of an independent Jewish state in Palestine would unquestionably relieve an immediate emergency. It would offer a way by which an eventual remedy for the major evil might be greatly expedited.

During recent decades, with the imposition of increasingly rigid restrictions upon immigration in all countries, the Jewish people in those regions where they have suffered persecution or discrimination have had no alternative but to continue where they were. With the creation of a national Jewish state the opportunity would at last be available to every Jew to find a home among his fellows in the Holy Land, should the conditions to which he is subjected prove intolerable.

There is here no question of divided loyalty. In those countries where the Jewish people have found happiness, the opportunity for advancement, and liberty free from discrimination, no body of citizens has proved more loyal nor contributed more to the land of their adoption. An independent Jewish Commonwealth of Palestine, however, affords the only definitive remedy for conditions that have today, in many parts of Europe, otherwise become incapable of solution within the forseeable future.

Could there be any nobler justification for remedial action by the United Nations if it is in fact to promote that "larger freedom" to which it has been dedicated by its Charter?

5

What the United Nations Has Done

THE SPECIAL SESSION of the General Assembly summoned at Great Britain's request met on April 28, 1947.

The problem of Palestine now laid before it represented by far the most serious as well as the most complicated issue with which the Assembly had had to deal during its short life. The smaller countries generally felt that the Security Council was crippled by the growing antagonism between the Soviet Union and the United States. They said openly that if the United Nations was to survive, the General Assembly, where no veto power could block action, must make use of the full authority granted it, and show that at a moment of world crisis the United Nations could act as well as talk.

The Assembly had, therefore, one great advantage. A large majority of the delegates were prepared to demonstrate that the town meeting of the world – as the Assembly had been called – was not only a forum where world public opinion could be freely voiced, but also an agency through which decisions could be translated into action.

The Special Session had another asset in its favor. Many delegates were men of outstanding ability, determined that the United Nations must succeed, and, because of their authority and experience, qualified to propose the methods best calculated to produce practical results. Prominent among these was Doctor Oswaldo Aranha, the former Foreign Minister of Brazil, who was elected President of the Assembly. Another was Doctor Herbert Evatt, the Australian Minister for External Affairs, one of the architects of the Charter and a recognized spokesman for the lesser Powers. The Canadian Under Secretary for Foreign Affairs, Lester B. Pearson, who was elected Chairman of the Assembly's Political and Security Committee, was a tower of strength. And by no means least were Ambassador Warren Austin and Ambassador Herschel Johnson representing the United States.

The first obstacle arose when the agenda came up for adoption. Five of the Arab states, Egypt, Iraq, Lebanon, Syria, and Saudi Arabia, demanded that the Assembly consider solely their proposal for "termination of the mandate over Palestine and the declaration of its independence." Their demand was rejected.

The next obstacle came from the insistence of the Arabs that since no Jewish state existed no representatives of the Jewish people should be heard. This restrictive interpretation of the Charter was unfortunately supported by the United States representative. The Assembly, however, voted to hear the Jewish Agency for Palestine – which had long enjoyed a semi-official status under the provisions of the British mandate – together with spokesmen for the Arab Higher Committee.

Two resolutions were then introduced, one by the United States and one by Argentina. Both proposed, as the British had asked, that the Assembly appoint a committee of inquiry with broad powers to recommend to the General Assembly a solution of the Palestine problem. The Argentine resolution, however, seconded by the Soviet Union, insisted that this committee of inquiry, like the Security Council, should be composed of the five major Powers and six lesser Powers. The United States proposed that the Palestine committee should consist exclusively of smaller Powers that had no direct interest in Palestine. After protracted debate the views of the United States were upheld. The Palestine Committee of Inquiry was then composed of representatives of Australia, Canada, Czechoslovakia, Guatemala, India, Iran, the Netherlands, Peru, Sweden, Uruguay and Yugoslavia.

In the final resolution adopted at this Special Session the Palestine Committee was given "the widest powers to ascertain and record facts, and to investigate any questions and issues relevant to the problem of Palestine, and to submit such proposals as it may consider appropriate for the solution of the problem of Palestine." The Committee was instructed "to give most careful consideration to the religious interests in Palestine of Islam, Judaism and Christianity."

Since the regular annual session of the Assembly was to meet the following September, the time available to the Palestine Committee was limited.

When the Committee signed its report on August 31 it had completed six weeks of intensive investigation of conditions within the Holy Land. Although the Arab Higher Committee had refused to co-operate, it had heard many prominent Arab leaders outside of Palestine. Members of the Committee had visited the European concentration camps where the Jewish refugees were still confined. With one exception its members measured up to their responsibilities. The Committee's majority and minority reports represented a painstaking and sincere effort to recommend solutions intended to further the highest interests of the inhabitants of Palestine and to eliminate the causes for further jeopardy to the peace of the Near East.

The minority plan, signed by representatives of India, Iran and Yugoslavia, proposed the creation of an independent federal state of Palestine after a brief transition period. The federation was to comprise two subordinate states, one Arab and one Jewish. There were to be two federal legislative bodies, one elected on the basis of proportional representation by all of the inhabitants of Palestine, and one giving equal representation to Arabs and to Jews. Jewish immigration into the Jewish state would, however, only be permitted during a period of three years – the total of such immigration to be determined by an agency of the United Nations – and thereafter immigration was to be regulated by the proposed federal government.

The majority plan signed by all of the remaining members of the Committee save the delegate of Australia – who refused to sign either plan – was altogether distinct. It proposed an economic union within Palestine of two politically independent states, one Jewish and one Arab. After a period of two years each state would become independent if it had adopted a constitution, agreed to guarantee religious and minority rights, and set up safeguards for the Holy Places. The City of Jerusalem was to be placed under a United Nations trusteeship. During the first two years one hundred and fifty thousand Jewish immigrants were to be permitted to enter the Jewish state, and, if the transitional period lasted for more than two years, sixty thousand additional Jewish immigrants would be admitted each year thereafter.

The minority report was summarily rejected by both the Jews and the Arabs. The Arabs insisted upon the immediate establishment of an independent Palestine in which the Jews should have no more than minority rights. To the Jews the minority plan was unacceptable because it would have deprived them of any opportunity ever to establish a free Jewish Commonwealth, and would have placed the ultimate control of immigration in the hands of the Arabs.

When the regular session of the General Assembly met in New York on September 17, 1947, the tides of controversy were again high.

The Assembly at this session was faced by many critical problems, such as the American proposals for elections in Korea and the creation of an interim committee of the Assembly. But Palestine overshadowed all others.

After an ad hoc committee had been set up to deal solely with the Palestine question, this body was charged with three obligations: to pass upon the majority and minority reports of the Palestine Committee of Inquiry, to determine the future status of Palestine as requested by Great Britain, and to deal with a renewed demand from the Arab states that the Assembly take action to bring about the termination of "the mandate over Palestine and the recognition of its independence as one state." At the outset of the debate there became evident one fact of outstanding significance. The United States and the Soviet Union, for the first time in the history of the United Nations, were in agreement on a matter of substance.

Secretary of State Marshall announced that the United States gave "great weight . . . to the recommendations . . . which have been approved by the majority" of the

Special Committee on Palestine. The Soviet Government expressed its conviction that the prime issue was to find the means of according the right of self-determination to Jews as well as to Arabs, and stated that because it realized that the respective desires of the two peoples could not be reconciled it would also support the majority plan proposing partition.

The British Government announced that it would support neither the majority nor the minority plan.

It was not long before it became plain that a great majority of the members of the United Nations favored the partition of Palestine and the other steps recommended in the majority report. A few changes in the proposed boundaries of the Jewish and Arab states were agreed upon. The Port of Jaffa was excluded from the Jewish state. The Town of Beersheba and a strip of the Negeb (the desert region in southern Palestine which the Jews hope through irrigation to use for large-scale resettlement) were transferred to Arab jurisdiction. With these modifications the partition plan was then accepted by the ad hoc committee.

At this stage the British Government announced that it would not take part in enforcing any plan that was not accepted by both Jews and Arabs. That meant that since the Arabs opposed any form of partition the British Administration in Palestine would refuse to co-operate in the enforcement of the partition plan.

A way around this major obstacle was sought through a program calling for the progressive withdrawal of the British armed forces up to August 1, 1948, and the final establishment of the proposed Arab and Jewish states before October 1, 1948. The partition plan was to be carried out by a United Nations Commission of five, again to be selected from among those smaller Powers that had no direct interest in Palestine. This commission in turn was to be guided not only by the instructions given it by the Assembly, but also by such additional instructions as the Security Council might consider necessary. The resolution which was then drafted for submission to the Assembly for final action contained these all-important provisions: the Security Council was requested "to take the necessary measures as provided for in the plan for its implementation"; and to *"determine as a threat to the peace, breach of the peace or act of aggression in accordance with Article 39 of the Charter any attempt to alter by force the settlement envisaged."*

The final effort of the Arab states to block the adoption by the Political Committee of the Assembly of the partition plan was overwhelmingly rejected.

But by this time the activities of all of those anti-Zionist groups that I have listed in an earlier chapter were beginning to have some effect upon the delegations. The Arabs were favored by other circumstances as well. While most of the Latin-American Republics, for example, strongly favored the partition of Palestine as the one solution that offered any hope of permanence, a few of the Latin-American delegates, in the belief that the influence of the lesser powers could best be insured by a working arrangement between the twenty Latin-American Republics and the six Arab states, were reluctant to take any action which might alienate the sympathies of the Arab countries. Both France and China were confronted with very real difficulties. China has a large Moslem population, and the Chinese Moslems demanded of their Government that it support no move that was opposed by their fellow Moslems in Arabia. France, faced with a Moslem majority in the French province of Algeria and in her protectorates of Morocco and Tunisia, was loath to take any action that might further stimulate unrest in French North Africa. The Government of the Netherlands, striving to construct a new federation of which the predominantly Moslem Netherlands East Indies would form a part, had to contend with a strongly pro-Arab feeling in Indonesia.

When the partition plan was finally introduced in a plenary meeting of the General Assembly on November 26 the outcome suddenly looked uncertain. Under the provisions of the Charter and the regulations of the Assembly a two-thirds majority was required for approval. It was known that among the Latin-American Republics Cuba was adamant in her opposition. It was also known that Argentina, Colombia, and Mexico would abstain from voting, and that certain other republics, notably Haiti, El Salvador, and Honduras, were inclined to follow the lead taken by Cuba. Several of the smaller nations of Western Europe were reluctant to take any definite position. Greece let it be known that her precarious situation in the Eastern Mediterranean made her unwilling to vote in favor of a resolution which would incur for her the hostility of her Arab neighbors. All of the Moslem countries were prepared to join the Arab states against partition.

In the light of later events it is important that there be no misunderstanding of the position that the United States assumed at that juncture. By direct order of the White House every form of pressure, direct and indirect, was brought to bear by American officials upon those countries outside of the Moslem world that were known to be either uncertain or opposed to partition. Representatives or intermediaries were employed by the White House to make sure that the necessary majority would at length be secured.

When the crucial moment arrived on November 29 the resolution providing for partition was finally approved by more than a two-thirds majority of the Assembly. Thirty-three nations voted in favor of it, thirteen against, and there were ten abstentions.

Before adjourning, the Assembly appointed Bolivia, Czechoslovakia, Denmark, Panama, and the Philippines members of the Commission on Palestine which was to serve as the agency of the Assembly in carrying out the partition plan. Doctor Ralph Bunche, a former official of the Department of State and one of the ablest members of the Secretariat of the United Nations, was appointed the Commission's Secretary General.

On December 9 the Security Council officially took cognizance of the partition plan. The Trusteeship Council simultaneously began preparing to administer the City of Jerusalem.

Agitation in all of the Arab states thereupon became intense. The Arab League met to concert measures by which the partition plan might be blocked. The nations that had voted for the plan were bitterly assailed. The denunciation was chiefly directed against the United States. What was far more significant were the military measures taken by the Arab Governments to prevent any implementation of partition. The authority of the United Nations was openly defied.

The Jewish leaders, on the other hand, while welcoming action by the Assembly that seemed to hold out to them the assurance that their hopes for an independent Jewish homeland would now be realized, were divided in their reactions. The more far-sighted, notably the leaders comprising the Executive Committee of the Jewish Agency, accepted the resolution of the Assembly, but with the clear-cut declaration that the plan proposed represented to them "an irreducible minimum." The extremists, however, rejected the decision that had been reached, and insisted that they would never be satisfied until the Jewish people controlled the whole of Palestine.

Disorders, violence, and bloodshed, which had temporarily halted while the Assembly was in session, once more flared up, and this time on a constantly increasing scale.

To every student of the Palestine problem, and to those who had followed the course of events in Palestine since the close of the war, the cardinal defect in the resolution adopted was its failure to provide before the Assembly adjourned any method for the enforcement of the partition plan should that prove necessary. It is true that the Assembly had requested the Security Council to "take the necessary measures, as provided for in the plan, for its implementation," and that the Security Council had further been called upon to "term as a threat to the peace, breach of the peace, or act of aggression . . . any attempt to alter by force the settlement envisaged by this resolution." The Security Council had not as yet, however, because of Soviet opposition, been able to establish the international police force envisaged in the Charter.

In an attempt to supply this salient requirement the American delegation, during the course of the debate, had urged the creation of an international constabulary of volunteers to maintain the peace in Palestine until the independence of the two new states had been firmly established. Because of the widespread belief among the other delegates that the Soviet Union and the two major Powers of the West would both suspect that such volunteers would include agents of the other, and that the resulting friction might have grave consequences, the American proposal received no support.

It is further true that the Assembly's plan included the stipulation that the new Jewish and Arab states should each "within the shortest time possible recruit an armed militia from the residents of that state sufficient in number to prevent further clashes," and that these forces were to be placed under the superior authority of the Palestine Commission.

But when the Assembly adjourned it was only too plain that nothing had been done to provide the force by which the authority of the United Nations could be maintained in Palestine or by which security to life and property could be guaranteed during the transition period which was shortly to commence. The urgency of the problem was emphasized by the declaration on December 11 of the British Colonial Secretary, Mr. Arthur Creech-Jones, that Great Britain would terminate her Palestine mandate on May 15, and complete the evacuation of her troops by the following first of August.

There should have been no doubt in the minds of any of the delegates in the Assembly that without military force at their command, the members of the Palestine Commission could neither carry out the terms of their mandate nor impose in Palestine respect for the authority of the United Nations.

It was idle for representatives of the United States later to protest that they had believed both Arabs and Jews would peacefully accept the Assembly's decision. Arab acquiescence might have been forthcoming had it been known that the United Nations had force available in case of need. But since it was known that not only was such force not available, but that no plans were even being considered to provide it, the Arab leaders were naturally soon convinced that they could embark upon a campaign of aggression with entire impunity.

Failing sufficient foresight on the part of the United States or of some other power to insist upon the creation of an ad hoc United Nations constabulary before the adjournment of the General Assembly, what became imperative was an initiative within the Security Council to bring about the creation of some United Nations police force to be sent to Palestine. No such initiative, however, was forthcoming.

With each week that passed Arab aggression became more flagrant. The Arab states adjacent to Palestine permitted the enlistment and arming of Arab volunteers within their boundaries. These troops received arms from several other Moslem countries. As Arab aggression against the Jews became more serious, the Jews of Palestine undertook acts of retaliation. The Haganah which, prior to the announcement of a Palestine settlement, had been the major Jewish resistance force, and which had co-operated with the Jewish Agency, constituted itself the nucleus of the Jewish militia envisaged in the partition plan. This militia, however, encountered severe curtailment of its activities by the British military administration. The United States made Jewish self-defense far more difficult by imposing an embargo upon the shipment of all arms to Palestine.

The British Government had officially declared that it regarded the decision of the Assembly as "the decision of a court of international opinion," and that for that opinion it would demonstrate "the greatest respect."

Yet there can be no question that from the date when the Assembly approved the partition plan, the attitude of every British official in Palestine was one of studied non-co-operation. And it must also be said that there is much confirmation of the report published in the *New York Herald Tribune,* on December 22, that "while higher

British policy is to treat Jews and Arabs alike, certain British police appear to be taking advantage of the disorder to settle scores marked up during the last two years."

By mid-January of 1948 the situation in Palestine was chaotic. The Arabs were openly receiving arms and munitions from every part of the Near East. The Jews were prevented from receiving weapons of defense because of the American embargo and because of the refusal of the British Government to permit arms to be imported from any other source. Not only was Arab aggression mounting, but armed and trained Arab forces were now invading Palestine from neighboring countries.

The Security Council continued to remain silent. Only the Palestine Commission of the United Nations expressed alarm.

On February 16 the Commission sent the Security Council an urgent report. It declared that "the authority and effectiveness of the United Nations" were deeply involved. It stated that it would "be unable to establish security and maintain law and order, without which it cannot implement the resolution of the General Assembly, unless military forces of adequate strength are made available to the Commission when the responsibility for the administration of Palestine is transferred to it."

The Commission then went into details. It listed the following factors as reasons for immediate action:

> (a) Organized efforts by strong Arab elements, inside and outside Palestine, to prevent the implementation of the Assembly's plan of partition and to thwart its objectives by threats and acts of violence, including armed incursion into Palestine territory;
>
> (b) Certain elements of the Jewish community in Palestine continue to commit irresponsible acts of violence

which worsen the security situation, although that community is generally in support of the recommendations of the Assembly;

(c) The added complication that the mandatory Power which remains responsible for law and order in Palestine until the termination of the mandate, is engaged in the liquidation of its administration and preparing for the evacuation of its troops.

Finally the Commission stated flatly that the British had obstructed every move the Commission had made for the purpose of organizing a local militia, but that even were such a militia to exist it would not be capable of resisting growing Arab aggression. Unless the Security Council provided an armed force to implement partition, the Commission announced that it could not "discharge its responsibilities on the termination of the mandate."

The gist of the Palestine Commission's appeal to the Security Council will be found in these words: "In the view of the Commission a basic issue of international order is involved. A dangerous and tragic precedent will have been established, if force, or the threat of the use of force, is to prove an effective deterrent to the will of the United Nations."

At length, almost three months after "the compelling need for prompt action," urged upon it by the Palestine Commission, had been glaringly apparent to even the most casual observer, the Security Council took up for consideration the case of Palestine.

The eyes of the world were turned upon the United States.

The American delegate, Ambassador Austin, on February 24, in an address to the Security Council, reviewed the partition plan and the course of events in Palestine. He declared on behalf of the United States that "in considering whether or not the situation in Palestine is a threat to international peace, the Security Council should consult with the United Kingdom which, as mandatory Power, is responsible for the protection of Palestine and the maintenance of internal order therein."

He then referred to that provision in the Assembly resolution which calls upon the Security Council to "determine as a threat to the peace, breach of the peace or act of aggression . . . an attempt to alter by force the settlement envisaged by this resolution." The American delegate insisted that "the Charter of the United Nations does not empower the Security Council to enforce a political settlement, whether it is pursuant to a recommendation of the General Assembly or of the Security Council itself."

After delivering himself of his Government's restrictive – and as will later be seen – wholly contradictory interpretation of the powers of the Security Council, Ambassador Austin proposed that the five permanent members of the Council "look at once into the question of the possible threats to international peace arising in connection with the Palestine situation," and that this committee of the five major Powers "consult with the Palestine Commission, the mandatory Power, and representatives of the principal communities of Palestine concerning the implementation of the General Assembly's recommendation."

This extraordinary declaration not unnaturally created a state of hopeless confusion. It was at once believed that the United States had abandoned its support for partition. Such charges were, however, promptly and emphatically denied by the American delegate, by the Secretary of State, and by the President of the United States himself.

During the following two weeks successive meetings of the delegates of the five major Powers were held. No decisions were reached, although the Soviet representative reiterated to the press his Government's unchanged view that partition afforded the one practical solution for the Palestine problem.

On March 18, because of his grave disquiet over the reports that the American Government had reversed its policy, Doctor Chaim Weizmann obtained an interview with the President of the United States. In the course of that interview President Truman assured Doctor Weizmann that the position of the United States had not changed in the slightest degree, and that the Government was also giving "very careful thought" to the desirability of lifting the arms embargo.

Less than twenty-four hours later the American delegate announced to the Security Council that his Government believed that partition could not be carried out except by force, and he therefore requested the Council immediately to instruct the Palestine Commission to suspend its efforts to implement the partition plan. He further proposed that another Special Session of the General Assembly be summoned in order that the United States might propose to it the establishment of a trusteeship over Palestine until such time as the Jews and Arabs could reach an agreement on the future of their country's government.

Whatever form the protestations of the American Government might still take there could now be no further doubt that the United States had completely reversed its policy, and had definitely abandoned the plan for the partition with economic union of Palestine.

6

American Policy

AMERICAN POLICY with regard to Palestine has in the past at times been governed by idealism, by humanitarian considerations, and by an enlightened grasp of the factors that make for world peace.

In dealing with the problem both Woodrow Wilson and Franklin Roosevelt had the broader viewpoint. They saw that the establishment of a National Homeland for the Jewish people, as promised by the Balfour Declaration, was not only an act of justice but that it would also serve to relieve economic and social pressures that were stimulating the growth of anti-Semitism in the Old World.

For far the greater part of the past thirty-one years, however, the policy of the United States toward Palestine has responded to the influence of politics or to that of large financial interests. Most recently it has been determined by the American armed services.

After the initial approval of the Balfour Declaration, and the announcement by President Wilson that the United States endorsed the establishment of an independent Jewish Commonwealth, this Government for many years showed little interest in Palestine once it had made certain that American rights would not be prejudiced by the British mandate. In 1924 the United States and the United Kingdom concluded a Convention in which these rights were guaranteed. Except, therefore, for such moral support as was given in the occasional pronouncements of American Presidents or in the resolutions adopted by the Congress, the United States took no positive steps to further the realization of the Balfour Declaration to which it had subscribed.

With the advent of the Second World War American policy once more became positive. Public opinion was aghast at Hitler's persecution of the Jews. The scope of the problem represented by the refugees began rapidly to be appreciated. To many Americans to whom Palestine had appeared to concern only the Zionists, the Arabs, and the British Government, it was now apparent that Palestine had become the only available refuge for many hundreds of thousands of otherwise homeless human beings.

Both major political parties inserted in their platforms in the campaign of 1944 planks calling for the exercise of American influence in expediting a Palestine settlement. The Congress adopted a Concurrent Resolution "that the United States shall use its good offices with the mandatory Power to the end that Palestine shall be opened for free entry of Jews into that country to the maximum of its agricultural and economic potentialities, and that there shall be full opportunity for colonization and development, and that they may freely proceed with the upbuilding of Palestine as the Jewish National Home, and, in association with all elements of the population, establish Palestine as a democratic Commonwealth in which all men, regardless of race or creed, shall have equal rights."

The terms of this resolution which urged the abrogation of restrictions on Jewish immigration, made it clear that the Congress envisaged a future Jewish majority in Palestine and the eventual creation of an independent Jewish state.

After the Second World War, President Truman's policy failed to contribute to the solution of the problem. His early demands for the immediate admission into Palestine of one hundred thousand refugees could hardly be other than barren. When these were supplemented by announcements that American troops would under no conditions be employed to maintain peace in Palestine, and that the American Government would share none of the other burdens that Britain would have to bear if the doors of Palestine were opened to large-scale immigration, the President's demands merely served to increase Mr. Bevin's obstinacy and to arouse general British irritation.

When the British Government at last decided to transfer the Palestine question to the United Nations, three influences that were destined to play a potent part in deciding American policy began to make themselves felt in Washington.

The first was that of the highest officials in the Department of Defense, to whom Palestine was nothing more than a problem in strategy. They saw the Near East as a probable base for future military operations against the Soviet Union, and as an area which contained perhaps as much as forty per cent of the oil resources of the world. Long before the conclusion of the war, the initiative had been taken by the Navy Department, strongly backed by Harold Ickes while he was Secretary of the Interior, in proposing the construction of pipelines to carry the oil produced in the Arabian fields to Mediterranean ports. To the strategy-planners these pipelines seemed to be American life-lines. Any policy that might induce the

Arab Governments to refuse their co-operation to the United States or to hinder American access to this oil seemed to them criminally stupid. A policy which demanded a Palestine solution that would fulfill the pledges given to the Jewish people, which would solve the otherwise insoluble problem of the European refugees, which would strengthen the authority of the United Nations, and at the same time settle a controversy that was threatening the peace of all of the Near East, was to them wholly mistaken so long as it might result in Arab disfavor and endanger American control of the oil fields.

It is hardly necessary to add that the lobbies maintained in Washington by the oil companies that had obtained concessions from the Arab Governments were giving enthusiastic support to the military standpoint.

The third influence was that of a number of officials in the Department of State. I have worked with some of these officials over a period of many years. I have complete faith in their integrity and respect for the sincerity of their beliefs. Mistaken as I believe them to be in their insistence that the friendship of the Arab world is of more value to this country than a just and lasting settlement of the Palestine controversy, I am confident that their views are based solely upon their conviction that the policies which they have so strongly urged upon the President and the Secretary of State are in the national interest.

In the opinion of these officials it is essential, in view of the aggressive intent of the Soviet Union, that no step be taken by the United States that would alienate the Arab peoples from this country. They consequently maintain that the United States should adopt as its own the policy of the British Government. They urge that no solution of the Palestine problem be imposed, and that no plan of settlement be sponsored by the United States unless it has been previously accepted by both Jews and Arabs. It is their viewpoint that in a Third World War Arab support is essential to the West, and that the only way in which that support can be obtained is by our permitting the Arabs to block any Palestine settlement which does not meet their approval.

When the problem of Palestine was presented to the Special Session of the Assembly of the United Nations in the spring of 1947, these three influences had already had some effect upon our policy. The position of the United States at this Session of the Assembly was far from being clear-cut in its support of the Jewish equities in Palestine.

It is true that the American delegate, Ambassador Johnson, in his address on April 30 made this statement:

> My Government, in preparing for this Special Session did so with the full realization of the importance of the Palestine problem not only to the parties most immediately concerned but to the whole world. We believe that this may be the last chance for the solving of this problem in a peaceful and fair manner. If this chance is missed, chaos and disorders might well result in Palestine of so serious a nature that that country would be ruined physically and morally.
>
> We are furthermore convinced that if the United Nations is to meet with success in its efforts to solve the Palestine problem the decision which it makes must be not only fair but one which has the support of world opinion and which is thought to be fair.
>
> It will be extremely difficult if not impossible to enforce any decision which does not rally the support of most of the peoples of the world.

This admirable analysis was, however, qualified by the specific reservation which the American delegate made on May 11. He then said, "I am not now arguing for the

Zionist state," and urged "that there should be nothing mandatory in the terms of reference and that everything should be permissive" in the instructions to be given to the Special Palestine Commission which the Assembly was to create.

The American position was in fact in sharp contrast with the unequivocal declaration of the Soviet delegate that the Soviet Government envisaged partition as presumably the only feasible solution that could be found in view of the unlikelihood that the Jews and Arabs could reach any agreement upon a settlement.

During the summer of 1947, while the Special Commission on Palestine was preparing its recommendations for a settlement, no indication was given by the United States Government of the course it would adopt when the question came before the Assembly for final adjudication.

When the regular session of the Assembly met, however, Secretary Marshall stated in his opening address that the United States gave "special weight" to the recommendation for partition contained in the majority report of the Special Commission. The United States thereupon began to evidence a sudden change of heart.

On October 12, Ambassador Johnson declared that while the American Government favored certain geographical and technical amendments it nevertheless fully supported "the basic principles of the unanimous recommendations" of the Special Commission, "and the majority plan which provides for partition and immigration."

In his address of November 22 before the Ad Hoc Committee of the General Assembly, Ambassador Johnson's statement of policy was still more categorical and much more far-reaching.

These statements made by the authorized representative of the United States must be quoted at some length if the underlying issues are to be understood in all of their implications.

In his statement of November 22, the American representative declared:

> We are dealing here with the means by which the United Nations might facilitate the transition of Palestine from the status of an international mandate to independence. No further period of tutelage is required in the case of this class of mandate. It has been unanimously agreed by the United Nations Special Committee of Inquiry on Palestine, and generally accepted as far as I am able to judge in this Assembly, that independence in Palestine should be attained as rapidly as possible. . . . The rôle of the United Nations is to be that of assisting in the actual transferral of authority from the mandatory Power to the independent states which it has been recommended shall succeed to the authority previously held by the United Kingdom in Palestine. . . . One of the principal difficulties with which the Ad Hoc Committee and the subcommittee have been faced is the situation created by the declaration of the mandatory Power [the refusal of the British Government to join in the enforcement of any plan which did not have the approval of both of the principal parties concerned].
>
> There is no present plan before the General Assembly of the United Nations with suggestions for a solution of the Palestine question, and none which has been presented or suggested, that could possibly meet that requirement. . . . We must postulate cooperation of the members of the United Nations, and cooperation in fact, not necessarily by way of implementation, but cooperation with the machinery which would be set up by the United Nations Commission on the part of the mandatory Power.
>
> The situation is an anomalous one. It was not contemplated in the Charter of the United Nations. It is a responsibility which falls squarely on the United Nations, not

> through its having sought that responsibility, but because of a unilateral declaration on the part of the mandatory Power that they were releasing their responsibility and requested the United Nations to make recommendations for solution of the problem. . . . My delegation will support and vote for the partition plan recommended to this Committee by Subcommittee 1. . . . The United Nations is the proper forum for the solution of this question, and, furthermore, the governments who believe in partition think that it is not perfect, but that it is humanly just and workable and, if adopted, will make a genuine and notable contribution to the solution of one of the most thorny political problems in the world today – a problem which I am certain that no delegation in the United Nations Assembly would like to admit even to themselves that the United Nations is incapable of solving. . . . I do not wish to take any more time of the Committee except to voice again the deep belief of my delegation that this partition plan, with all its imperfections, offers the most practicable and most just present solution of the Palestine problem.

This statement of American policy was positive. It was unequivocal. It differed from this Government's position four months before in its categorical assertion that the United States believed that the partition plan recommended by the General Assembly was "the most practicable and most just present solution of the Palestine problem."

The explanation for the change in the attitude of the Administration is that public opinion had made itself felt. The recommendations formulated by the Assembly had won a wide measure of popular support. It was realized that any prolonged continuation of chaotic conditions in Palestine would involve a very real danger of open warfare. In that case the Soviet Union might legitimately insist upon using armed force to end hostilities in a region adjacent to her own sphere of interest on the ground that her security was endangered, and that the United Nations had taken no restraining measures. There was widespread recognition that clear-cut action by the United Nations would be the most likely means of procuring a lasting settlement, and of forestalling any entrance by Russia into the Mediterranean.

The advocates within the Congress of such a settlement were numerous and influential. Together with certain of his personal advisers, they represented to President Truman the need for a positive policy. Nor can it be denied that politics played a considerable part in determining the action of the White House. While Americans of the Jewish faith were still divided, many Jews who had previously opposed the objectives of the Zionists now believed that the settlement recommended by the Assembly offered the one hope of providing new homes for the European refugees. Jewish support for the partition plan became overwhelming. In several of the larger cities the political influence of this body of American citizens was considerable and their allegiance was a matter of more than passing concern to a President whose desire for reelection was well known. Neither the objections of the armed services nor those coming from the Department of State were for the moment able to prevail. To all appearances the decision reached by the President was final. There was every reason for foreign governments and for American public opinion to believe that the United States would assume the same kind of forthright leadership in implementing the partition plan as that which it had undertaken in persuading the Assembly to adopt that plan.

During the following two months there was no evidence that American policy was undergoing any change.

The continued silence of Washington in the face of open Arab aggression, and notwithstanding the urgent pleas of the Palestine Commission for remedial action, however, gave rise to some suspicions that this Government had become at least lukewarm. But these suspicions were at first allayed by repeated official assurances that the Government stood foursquare behind the partition plan.

A material change had, however, already taken place behind the scenes. During the brief time since the Assembly had approved the plan, relations between the Soviet Union and the United States had rapidly deteriorated. The decision of the Kremlin to sabotage the European Recovery Program, the campaign conducted by the Communists in Italy and in France, Soviet activities in Scandinavia, China, Korea, and Iran, the elimination of the last vestige of popular government in the Balkans, Soviet support for the rebellion against the constitutional government of Greece, climaxed by the seizure of Czechoslovakia and the demand upon Finland for a military alliance, all combined to make it seem that the Soviet program for aggressive expansion was being accelerated, and accelerated to a point where resistance by the United States and by the Western European Powers might before long have to be made evident by more than mere words of reprobation.

To the arguments earlier advanced by the President's military and naval advisers against American support for the partition plan, there were now available the added arguments that because of Arab resistance partition could only be imposed by force; that since the Security Council had as yet no international police force at its disposal, only the British, the Russians, and the Americans could supply the troops needed, and that the Soviet Union would unquestionably demand equal participation with the Western Powers, if the United Nations sent an armed force to Palestine. It was pointed out that, were American and Russian troops both despatched to Palestine, precisely the same difficulties would arise as those already encountered in Korea, and that once Russian troops were in Palestine there was no means of knowing when, if ever, they might withdraw, or how much further they might try to go. It was further argued that in view of the new crisis the United States must be assured that the territory of Palestine would be available as a base for the air and ground forces of the Western Powers.

These arguments were on their face quite plausible. They were, of course, bolstered by the views of the Department of State, and by the representations of the American oil companies that if the United States continued to press for partition, the oil of the Near East would be unavailable for our national defense and equally unavailable to the countries of Western Europe that must have access to this source of supply if the European Recovery Program was to succeed.

To an Administration which had no convictions with respect to the ethical values that Palestine represented, that neither then nor later showed any sign of grasping the broader implications inherent in the settlement of the Palestine problem, and that had long since been dominated by the military mentality, the arguments so advanced finally proved conclusive. The climax came after the Palestine Commission rendered its special report to the Security Council on February 16 when it urgently pointed out that conditions in Palestine had reached such a pass that the Commission had no hope of carrying out the responsibilities entrusted to it unless the Security Council provided the force by which peace could be restored to Palestine.

A week later Ambassador Austin addressed the Security Council. He there maintained that although the Council was required by the Charter to act should it determine that there was any "threat to the peace, breach of the peace, or act of aggression" in Palestine, the Security Council was not empowered by the Charter to enforce partition.

To the man in the street this represented a reversal of policy. But when the American delegate to the United Nations, the Secretary of State, and the President of the United States were once more asked whether this Government was withdrawing its support from the partition plan, the replies given were once more categorical: the United States had no thought of modifying, much less of reversing, its announced policy.

On March 5 the Security Council agreed to an American proposal that the five major Powers consult. But in their discussions it was soon plain that the United States not only had no suggestions to offer for the implementation of the partition plan, but that, by urging that avenues of conciliation between Jews and Arabs should be once more explored, its chief objective was further delay. This impression was strengthened when it became known that due to American pressure within the Trusteeship Council consideration of the draft statute for the proposed international zone of Jerusalem had been suspended for six weeks, although under the provisions of the Assembly resolution the final date for the approval by the Trusteeship Council of such a statute had been fixed for April 29.

The representations made to the White House and to the Department of State that the prestige of the United States was at stake, that the course pursued by the Jewish Agency, and by the other more moderate elements in Palestine, had been followed only because of their trust in the good faith of this country, and that at this late date a reversal of its policy by the United States would gravely undermine popular confidence throughout the world in the United Nations, were scarcely heeded.

On March 19 in a new declaration to the Security Council Ambassador Austin made the remarkable pronouncement that

> a unilateral decision by the United Kingdom to terminate the Palestine mandate cannot automatically commit the United Nations to responsibility for governing that country. We think it clear that the United Nations does not succeed to administrative responsibility for Palestine merely because the latter is a mandate. . . . No proposal was made by the United Kingdom to the General Assembly that the United Nations itself undertake responsibility for the government of Palestine. . . . The [partition] plan proposed by the General Assembly was an integral plan which would not succeed unless each of its parts could be carried out. There seems to be general agreement that the plan cannot now be implemented by peaceful means. From what has been said in the Security Council, it is clear that the Security Council is not prepared to go ahead with efforts to implement this plan in the existing situation. . . . My Government believes that a temporary trusteeship for Palestine should be established under the Trusteeship Council of the United Nations to maintain the peace and to afford the Jews and Arabs of Palestine further opportunity to reach an agreement regarding the future government of that country. Such a United Nations trusteeship would, of course, be without prejudice to the character of the eventual political settlement which we hope can be achieved without long delay.

In concluding his declaration Ambasador Austin urged the convocation of an immediate special session of the

General Assembly in order that it might consider these recommendations of the United States.

The proposals that this declaration embodied represented a total reversal of the position assumed by the United States three months before. They rendered inexplicable the denials of such a reversal of policy that the Administration had continued to reiterate until only a few hours before Ambassador Austin's announcement. Leaving aside for the time being the effect upon the authority of the United Nations which this exposition of the American interpretation of the Charter must have, if, as the American delegate stated, the United Nations had assumed no responsibility for Palestine when Britain announced her decision to terminate her mandate, why had the Assembly a year before decided to recommend a settlement? Why, after protracted investigation and full debate, had it undertaken to approve by a large majority a plan for the partition of Palestine? Why had the United States exercised the full measure of its influence in order to secure the approval of the Assembly for the partition plan? And why had Ambassador Johnson, speaking in the name of the United States, declared to the Assembly only four months before: "The United Nations is the proper forum for the solution of this question. . . . No further period of tutelage is required in the case of this class of mandate. . . We are dealing here with the means by which the United Nations might facilitate the transition of Palestine from the status of an international mandate to independence"?

These questions and many others were asked of the American Government by the press and radio, and by outstanding citizens, in the United States and throughout the rest of the world the following day.

The basic issues could not have been more cogently

stated than they were by the *New York Times,* a newspaper traditionally opposed to Zionism, on March 21:

> Three things need to be said and to be said at once concerning the present shift of American policy on Palestine. The first is that it comes as a climax to a series of moves which has seldom been matched for ineptness in the handling of any international issue by an American Administration. The second is that it is a plain and unmistakable surrender to the threat of force. And the third is that it holds little promise of being able to avoid the very hazards which it is intended to circumvent.

The Administration had not anticipated the unanimity nor the bitterness of the condemnation with which its policy shift was met.

The first attempt at palliation was undertaken by Secretary Marshall. But to his explanation that "vital elements of our national security" contributed to the decision reached by the Government, the *New York Herald Tribune,* in an editorial of March 22, accurately voiced the general reaction:

> If it is true that the maintenance of peace in the Near East is essential to America's interests does the proposed trusteeship supply any greater assurance of stability than the enforcement of partition? . . . The implications that partition is only useful if it can be achieved peaceably leaves the whole Palestine dilemma virtually insoluble. To urge, as the Secretary of State has done, that trusteeship may produce an "agreed settlement" – the general goal of years of effort – is painfully unrealistic. Force will have to be used to maintain even the semblance of order in the Holy Land; force will almost inevitably have to be used to reach a settlement that will have any chance of permanence. The day of reckoning is only postponed. And to what end?

And this same editorial of the *New York Herald Tribune* also raised a question that was being generally asked:

> Although the United States is now committed to trusteeship, Russia retains virtually all of her freedom of action. Her support for partition was brought forward with the greatest caution; she can either use it as a club to beat the East, or drop it if the United States becomes embroiled with the Arabs over trusteeship.

In a vain attempt to still the ever-mounting tide of criticism President Truman issued a public statement on March 26. He said:

> We could not undertake to impose this solution on the people of Palestine by the use of American troops both on Charter grounds and as a matter of national policy.
>
> The United Kingdom has announced its firm intention to abandon its mandate in Palestine on May 15. Unless emergency action is taken there will be no public authority in Palestine on that date capable of preserving law and order. Violence and bloodshed will descend upon the Holy Land. Large scale fighting among the people of that country will be the inevitable result. Such fighting would infect the entire Middle East and could lead to consequences of the gravest sort involving the peace of this nation and of the world. . . . If the United Nations agrees to a temporary trusteeship we must take our share of the necessary responsibility. Our regard for the United Nations, for the peace of the world, and for our own self-interest does not permit us to do less.

Such a statement, incoherent, contradictory, and inaccurate as it must be regarded under even the most favorable interpretation, increased popular confusion and dismay.

Surely the chief reason why, as the President said, there

would be no public authority in Palestine on March 15 which could preserve law and order, was this Government's failure, when the partition plan was adopted, to take steps to see that the Security Council created an international police force to keep the peace when the British mandate ended. If the United States, according to the President, was in its own view prevented, "on Charter grounds," from co-operating in the enforcement of the partition plan, why should the United States be free to co-operate in imposing the establishment of a trusteeship? Yet the President declared, "we must take our share of the necessary responsibility" if a trusteeship were imposed. If "violence and bloodshed" were to descend upon the Holy Land if partition was imposed, why was a far greater measure of violence and bloodshed not to be expected if the United States joined in imposing a trusteeship upon Palestine? For if partition were enforced the Jews of Palestine would support the plan of settlement recommended by the Assembly and would actively co-operate in seeing that it was carried out. If a trusteeship were imposed, however, the forces that might be sent to Palestine would be met not only by Arab resistance but also by Jewish resistance, for the Jews had at once declared that they would oppose by force any plan of settlement that did not immediately give them their promised independence.

The American people are idealists. They stand for justice and fair dealing. They have an immense pride in the good name of their nation. They believe that their country must respond to a call for moral leadership. In their great majority they now realize that world peace can only come through collective security, and they are not blind to the significance of that series of events – all of them so easily avoided – that led up to the last war, which Winston Churchill so rightly calls "The Unnecessary War."

Many among them have felt a sense of deep personal humiliation and of profound discouragement as they have witnessed these recent phases of their Government's foreign policy. They have shared in the bitterness expressed in these words of Thomas Mann:

> This surrender to brazen Arab threats is the most humiliating and shocking political event since the democracies betrayed Czechoslovakia in 1938. . . . It makes us realize — with considerable alarm — how far the ideals of democracy, truth, liberty and justice, have been degraded. . . .
>
> Has anyone considered the blow this deplorable decision has dealt the authority of the United Nations and its ability to maintain world peace? . . .
>
> Perhaps the indignant outcries of a moral world will lead to a revision of the shameful decision. If not, it proves that the immense disappointment of all hopes for a better, juster world has turned to apathy, to a numbed submission of mankind to the threatening disaster.

7

What We Could Have Done

IN ITS RESOLUTION of November 29, 1947, recommending the partition and economic union of Palestine, the Assembly had requested that:

(*a*) The Security Council take the necessary measures as provided for in the plan for its implementation;

(*b*) The Security Council consider, if circumstances during the transitional period require such consideration, whether the situation in Palestine constitutes a threat to the peace. If it decides that such a threat exists, and in order to maintain international peace and security, the Security Council should supplement the authorization of the General Assembly by taking measures, under Articles 39 and 41 of the Charter, to empower the United Nations Commission, as provided in this resolution, to exercise in Palestine the functions which are assigned to it by this resolution;

(*c*) The Security Council determine as a threat to the peace, breach of the peace, or act of aggression, in accordance with Article 39 of the Charter, *any attempt to alter by force the settlement envisaged by this resolution.*

In the preamble of this resolution it was specifically stated that a compelling reason for its adoption was the Assembly's decision *"that the present situation in Pales-*

tine is one which is likely to impair the general welfare and friendly relations among nations."

During the years since the end of the war, Palestine had been plunged into a state of anarchy. Violence and bloodshed had become the rule and were no longer the exception. Arab rejection of any form of settlement that would not give the Arabs complete control was a foregone conclusion. By the autumn of 1947 there was incontrovertible evidence that the Arabs of Palestine would be joined by their Arab neighbors in armed resistance to such a settlement as that recommended by the Assembly unless they were convinced that the United Nations was determined and prepared to enforce its will.

Spokesmen for the American Government made it appear in their public utterances that when the partition plan was adopted, the opinion that prevailed in the Assembly was that persuasion would be sufficient to induce Jews and Arabs peacefully to accept the implementation of the partition plan. Many also alleged that the delegates were misled by Jewish insistence that the Arab threats of violence were only "bluff."

These assertions were unfounded.

Many delegates then believed that the Arab threats would only prove to be "bluff" if the Arabs knew that the Security Council had established an international constabulary of adequate size, that it would be at once despatched to Palestine to keep the peace, and to resist, as the Assembly had requested of the Security Council, "any attempt to alter by force the settlement envisaged by this resolution."

Few could, however, have imagined, in view of the passions that had been aroused, and in the light of conditions already then existing in Palestine, that the partition plan could be carried out if the United Nations were unwilling to lift a finger to make its authority respected, or to show itself impotent to put down by force any resistance to its plan to remedy a situation that it had declared was "likely to impair the general welfare and friendly relations among nations." No delegate to the Assembly was under any illusions in that regard.

The Government of the United States was fully aware of the implications inherent in the partition plan. In his address of April 30, 1947, Ambassador Johnson had declared "it will be extremely difficult, if not impossible, to *enforce* any decision which does not rally the support of most of the people of the world." On November 22 he had insisted "that no delegation in the United Nations Assembly would like to admit even to themselves that the United Nations is incapable of solving" the Palestine problem.

It was precisely because the United States recognized that the United Nations had an inescapable obligation to "enforce" the settlement agreed upon, that the American delegation submitted to the Assembly its plan for the establishment by the United Nations of an international volunteer force to preserve the peace in Palestine.

It is true that the American proposal for an international volunteer force met with little favor from the other delegations and was soon dropped by the United States. While this proposal avoided the difficulties involved in the creation of a police force composed of military contingents from the larger member states, its underlying dangers were apparent. The antagonism between the Soviet Union and the Western Powers made it inevitable that each would have suspected the other of trying to make such a force subservient to its individual interests. There would undoubtedly also have been an effort on the part of both Jews and Arabs to pack it with their own followers. Had it been determined that both Jews and Arabs were to be excluded, what standards could have been set up to insure the enlistment of only such volunteers as were not subservient to the interests of some major Power? Presumably many of the anti-communist Poles who had been given refuge in Italy or Great Britain would desire to enlist. They would naturally have been suspect to the Soviet Government. The Western Powers would equally naturally have been suspicious of volunteers from Yugoslavia and Bulgaria. It was unlikely that a sufficient number of volunteers from such neutral countries as the Scandinavian states or Switzerland could have been found to make up the force needed. Superficially desirable as the American proposal may have seemed, the practical difficulties involved made it impracticable.

The Security Council, because of Russian intransigence, had not yet been able to agree upon the establishment of the permanent international police force required by the Charter. To meet the request of the Assembly some ad hoc force would have to be created. The simplest solution, a force combining contingents from the major Powers, was clearly unacceptable. The joint occupation of Korea by the Soviet Union and the United States had already proved that only increased tension could be anticipated from a repetition of that experiment. With the ever-growing contest for supremacy in the Eastern Mediterranean, neither the United States nor the Soviet Union could be expected to agree to the policing of Palestine by an expeditionary force of the other. France had few troops available, nor would the Soviet Union have agreed if she had. The British Government had declared repeatedly that under no conditions would British troops be used to impose any settlement by force, and that in no event would British troops remain in Palestine after August 1, 1948.

Under these circumstances only one solution was feasible. That solution was the creation by the Military Staff Committee of the Security Council, under its technical command, but subject to the orders of the Palestine Commission, of a force composed of contingents from the regular military establishments of a sufficient number of the small nations that had no direct interest in Palestine. This solution would have required the payment by the major Powers of the costs involved. It would, however, not have been subject to political or strategic objections. It would have presented the intermediary and lesser Powers in the United Nations with an opportunity to assume their share of responsibility for solving a problem which threatened world peace, and for maintaining the authority of the United Nations upon which their own future security so greatly depended. The assumption of these responsibilities might not have been welcomed. But such nations, for example, as Brazil and Mexico, Sweden and Norway, the Netherlands and Belgium, could have well afforded to make the relatively small sacrifice that this might have represented.

Had the United States made any serious attempt, as the delegation of New Zealand so earnestly did, before the Assembly adjourned on November 30, to convince the other member nations that the task of the Assembly could only be regarded as half-finished unless it came to some definitive understanding with the Security Council upon a method of enforcing partition, should enforcement prove necessary, there can be little doubt that the creation of such a constabulary as that suggested could have been agreed upon. There is no valid ground for the assertion that the Soviet Government would at that time have vetoed the establishment of such an international force. There is no basis for the presumption that the small Powers would have proved recalcitrant. There is every reason to believe that had the Arabs known that such an international force was in process of creation, and would be despatched to Palestine to replace the British troops as these were withdrawn, the Arabs would neither have committed the acts of aggression of which they were later guilty, nor have dared openly to defy the United Nations.

It is reported that the failure of the United States to take a step which foresight demanded was due to its belief that it could still persuade the British Government to continue its military occupation of Palestine, and maintain order, until the partition plan had been carried out and that this arrangement would avoid many undesirable complications. The Defense authorities in Washington of course also insisted that any military force composed of small contingents from several nations, trained under diverse military systems and speaking different languages, would have proved unwieldy and ineffective. This was surely another instance of where the perfect is the enemy of the good. Such a solution would necessarily present many difficult technical problems. But if no other solution could be found, was it not far better for such a force, with all of its possible defects, to be employed by the Security Council, than for the United Nations to appear impotent, to have the tragedy of Palestine become daily more desperate, and to have the United States find itself in a position as profoundly humiliating as any in its history?

This failure of the United States to assume leadership in procuring the establishment of an international force to maintain peace in Palestine was rendered far more serious by its imposition of an embargo upon all shipments of arms to that country. This was announced on December 6, 1947, only one week after the Assembly had adjourned. Under the circumstances this could only serve further to endanger the precarious position of the Jews.

The partition plan provided for the creation in the proposed Jewish and Arab states of national militias to maintain order within their respective territories. The Arabs refused to establish any militia. But the Jewish resistance force, the Haganah, offered a nucleus for the militia in the Jewish state. The Jews had assumed that the United Nations would send some international force to maintain order and to protect the inhabitants of Palestine from aggression. Yet when it began to be apparent that the sole protection that the Jews were to have was that which their own armed forces could supply, they found themselves deprived of any chance to obtain the arms and ammunition that they desperately needed from the United States. British import embargoes prevented them from securing arms from sources nearer at hand. At the same time it was notorious that the Arabs in Palestine were getting all of the military equipment they needed from the neighboring Arab governments, and that a large part of this was being sold to these governments by Great Britain.

Under these conditions the maintenance by the United States of its arms embargo represents an act of flagrant injustice for which there can be no extenuation.

These fatal errors of omission and of commission on the part of the United States, together with the antagonistic attitude consistently pursued by the British authorities in the Holy Land, were directly responsible for the progressive and rapid deterioration in the Palestine situation.

There could be no more impartial or accurate presentation of the situation to which all of this had given rise than that presented in the Report of the Palestine Commission on April 14:

> The general policy of the mandatory Power has been not to take any measure which might be construed as involving it in the implementation of the Assembly's resolution. It did not accept the provision of the resolution calling for a progressive transfer of authority to the Commission; it insisted on retaining undivided control of Palestine until the termination of the mandate; and informed the Commission that it "would not regard favorably" the arrival of the Commission in Palestine earlier than a fortnight before the date of the mandate.
>
> More important still, Arab elements, both inside and outside of Palestine, have exerted organized, intensive effort toward defeating the purposes of the resolution of the General Assembly. To this end, threats, acts of violence, and infiltration of organized, armed, uniformed Arab bands in Palestine territory have been employed. As early as the 16th of February the Commission, in its first special report to the Security Council, stated that "powerful Arab interests, both inside and outside Palestine, are defying the resolution of the General Assembly and are engaged in a deliberate effort to alter by force the settlement envisaged therein."
>
> The organized efforts of the Arab elements to prevent the partition of Palestine; the determined efforts of Jews to insure the establishment of the Jewish State as envisaged by the resolution; and the fact that the mandatory Power, engaged in the liquidation of its administration and the vacation of its troops, has found it impossible fully to contain the conflict, have led to virtual civil war in Palestine; to a steady deterioration in administration and security in the territory; and to the imminence of widespread chaos, starvation, strife and bloodshed on a scale hitherto unknown.

> . . . In the view of the Commission the dominant fact is, however, that in the absence of forces adequate to restore and maintain law and order in Palestine following the termination of the mandate, there will be administrative chaos, starvation, widespread strife, violence and bloodshed in Palestine.

But grave as these errors in American policy have been, it was doubtful that they could have so far-reaching an effect upon the vital interests of the United States as the declarations of policy made by this Government through its representatives at the February 24 and March 19 meetings of the Security Council.

At those meetings Ambassador Austin announced that the United States so interpreted the United Nations Charter as to imply that the Security Council had no right to comply with one of its most vital obligations, and an obligation that had already previously been confirmed. He said:

> The Charter of the United Nations does not empower the Security Council to enforce a political settlement whether it is pursuant to a recommendation of the General Assembly or of the Council itself.
>
> What this means is this: The Council under the Charter can take action to prevent aggression against Palestine from outside. The Council by these same powers can take action to prevent a threat to international peace and security from inside Palestine. But this action must be directed solely to the maintenance of international peace. The Council's action, in other words, is directed to keeping the peace and not to enforcing partition.

By that declaration the Government of the United States announced a reversal of its policy on Palestine. It thereby also announced a complete reversal of its position, as earlier defined, with respect to the power and authority of the Security Council.

The import of these declarations upon the future of the United Nations could hardly be overestimated.

At the same time this announcement was in open contradiction of the stand taken by the United States when it pressed for the adoption of the partition resolution. For if the Charter did not empower the Security Council to enforce a political settlement, on what ground could the United States have been warranted in supporting and in voting for a resolution which called upon the Security Council to determine as an "act of aggression . . . any attempt to alter by force the settlement envisaged by this resolution"?

This reversal of American policy was subjected publicly to a devastating analysis by Benjamin Cohen. Mr. Cohen, who had resigned as Counselor of the Department of State a few months before, had played a leading part in the earlier formulation of American policy in the United Nations. He was entitled to speak with peculiar authority.

Mr. Cohen pointed out that Ambassador Austin's pronouncement cast doubt on the authority of the Security Council to remove a threat to world peace by requiring the parties to some dispute to accept a political settlement of their differences. As he put it, "Those implications would go far to make the Charter impotent, and to relieve the members of the United Nations of any real responsibility thereunder. In these critical days it is not in our interest or in the interest of freedom and law in the world for us to read the life out of the Charter of the United Nations."

Mr. Cohen emphasized that the position now taken

by the United States represented a complete abandonment of this Government's previous position: "Heretofore the approach of the American Government to the United Nations has been not to inquire what we legally and technically are obligated to do, but what we legally and practically can do to make the United Nations effective."

He cited several specific instances as evidence.

For example, the United States, in the spring of 1946, when Iran was threatened with Soviet aggression, officially announced that even though a Soviet veto might be imposed on action by the Security Council, it would nevertheless defend the purposes, principles, and policies of the United Nations.

What represented an even more clear-cut instance of this reversal of American policy regarding the powers of the United Nations was that afforded by the case of Trieste.

It had been largely due to American initiative that the Security Council had accepted the responsibilities which the Italian Peace Treaty conferred upon it in Trieste. The Security Council recognized at that time, in the case of Trieste, that it was authorized to act, not only under Article 39 of the Charter with reference to specific threats to the peace, but also under Article 24, which gives the Security Council primary responsibility for the maintenance of international peace and security. The Security Council acted upon the basis of a formal legal opinion communicated to it by the Secretary General of the United Nations. In this opinion it was specifically stated that "the Security Council is not restricted to the specific powers set forth in Chapters VI, VII, VIII and XII of the Charter but is held to have powers commensurate with its responsibilities in the field of the maintenance of international peace and security."

In this question of Trieste the United States had warmly endorsed the interpretation of the powers of the Security Council as defined by the Secretary General. Now it denied that the Security Council had the authority to impose or enforce a political settlement under the terms of Article 39 of the Charter, even though the Security Council deemed such a settlement essential to the maintenance or restoration of international peace and security.

The more purely legal aspects of the problem were set forth in Mr. Cohen's published statement:

> At the present time the Security Council . . . is dealing with a recommendation which has not only been supported by more than two-thirds of the member states voting, but it has been accepted by the mandatory Power, the only sovereign state having substantive rights in Palestine. So far as the authority of the Security Council to assist in the implementation of the plan is concerned, the Palestine plan created by the resolution voted by the General Assembly and accepted by the United Kingdom is not essentially different legally from the plan for the free territory of Trieste created by the peace treaty and accepted by Italy. The maintenance of peace in each of these countries is significantly related to the maintenance of international peace and security. Article 24 of the Charter conferring upon the Security Council primary responsibility for international peace and security, is as much applicable to the one plan as to the other.

But the essence of the whole question could not be better expressed than in this final quotation from Mr. Cohen's statement:

> In a practical world the problem of peace and the problem of settlement are frequently one and inseparable . . .
>
> In truth, peace cannot be maintained and war averted without regard to the question of the threats to the peace.
>
> If the Charter is to live we must not exalt the letter which

killeth and destroy the spirit which giveth life. To paraphrase the words of Chief Justice Marshall, we must remember that the Charter was intended to endure for ages to come and to be adapted to the various crises in human affairs.

By the narrow and restrictive interpretation now given by the American Government to the Charter, thus reversing the position it had taken when the broader interpretation had seemed to serve its own interests, the United States could not fail to be regarded by the other member countries as seeking to use the United Nations as an instrument of its own national policy. In the case of Trieste the United States had found it expedient to maintain that the powers of the Security Council were not limited to the specific rights entrusted to it by the Charter, but were commensurate with the Council's responsibilities in the field of "the maintenance of international peace and security." In the case of Palestine, because it seemed momentarily expedient, the United States on the contrary held that the Security Council had no authority to undertake any responsibilities save those specifically listed in the Charter.

By no means the least potent of the causes that contributed to the collapse of the League of Nations had been the successive attempts of Great Britain and of France to use the League of Nations to serve their own selfish ends, rather than for the purpose of furthering the cause of collective security and the welfare of the community of nations.

Because of its lack of foresight, because of its shortsighted concentration upon considerations of expediency, and because of its vacillation, the United States had vastly complicated the problem of implementing the partition plan with which the United Nations was confronted in March 1948.

There were inherent in partition dangers that could not be minimized. But those dangers were equally implicit, and in many ways far graver, in the plan for trusteeship which the United States now proposed. There can be little question that even as late as March, 1948, had the United States resumed its earlier support for the plan of partition and economic union, the way could readily have been found by the Security Council for the implementation of that plan, and, through prompt action, for the elimination of many of the dangers by which the Administration in Washington was obsessed.

8

What Can Still Be Done

When the Special Assembly requested by the United States convened on April 16, 1948, the prestige of the United Nations had reached its lowest ebb. International confidence in the capacity of the American Government to offer constructive leadership in an attempt to find a way out of the Palestine imbroglio, for which it was chiefly responsible, was painfully lacking.

As the delegates assembled, the general sensation of futility and even of despair that prevailed was heightened by several factors.

The general pessimism was indicated by the absence of all of those outstanding statesmen who had contributed so much to the success of the session of the preceding autumn.

The unwillingness or inability of the United States to influence the organization of the session so as to secure at least an able and impartial direction of the Assembly's deliberations was evidenced when elections for the President of the Assembly and for the principal executive officers of the conference took place.

At the preceding sessions of the Assembly, Doctor Oswaldo Aranha of Brazil had presided with impartiality, courage, and singular ability. He was now replaced by Doctor Arce of Argentina, elected by a combination formed by the Arab states and the Latin-American Republics, which had at the last moment been joined by the United States itself. At the prior session of the Assembly the Argentine Government had refused to vote for the partition plan, and the Jewish leaders strongly believed that the Argentine Government, and Doctor Arce in particular, would favor no step by the Assembly which recognized the justice of their cause.

Doctor Tsiang of China, elected Chairman of the all-important Political Committee, was, of course, bound by the position officially taken by his Government, that, because of the extensive Moslem population in China, the Chinese Government would refuse to support any settlement of the Palestine question that was not acceptable to the Arabs.

From the outset it was therefore plain that the organization of the session would be weighted heavily on the Arab side.

The prospects for any remedial action by the Assembly were further darkened by the course of events in Palestine, by the accomplished facts which now existed with respect to that country, and by the confused and self-contradictory statements that continued to be made by representatives of the American Government.

The United Nations Commission on Palestine reported on April 17 that the refusal of the British authorities to co-operate in any way in providing for the progressive transfer of administration to the Palestine Commission had had these consequences: on May 15, barely four weeks later, the Commission would be faced with responsibility for the administration of Palestine although the British had prevented it from making any prior preparations; for the same reason the Commission had been unable to determine the boundaries of the Arab and Jewish states, or of the City of Jerusalem, over which, under the partition plan, the United Nations was to exercise control; to set up any political organizations in Palestine, or, what was still more urgent, to create the armed militias which, under the partition plan, were essential for the defense of the inhabitants.

The Commission pointed out that Jerusalem was already in grave danger of destruction from the conflict in progress, that food shortages throughout Palestine were already desperate, and that administrative chaos and total civil war loomed in the immediate future. It declared that notwithstanding the terms of the Assembly's resolution of November 29, 1947, the Commission had received neither "guidance nor instructions" from the Security Council in response to its urgent appeals.

It concluded its report with these charges:

> The Commission, therefore, has the duty to report to the General Assembly that the armed hostility of both Palestinian and non-Palestinian Arab elements, the lack of cooperation from the mandatory Power, the disintegrating security situation in Palestine, and the fact that the Security Council did not furnish the Commission with the necessary armed assistance, are the factors which have made it impossible for the Commission to implement the Assembly's resolution.
>
> The steadily deteriorating situation in Palestine leads to the inescapable conclusion that, in the absence of forces adequate to restore and maintain law and order in Palestine following the termination of the mandate, there will be administrative chaos, starvation, widespread strife, violence and bloodshed in Palestine, including Jerusalem. These calamitous results for the people of Palestine will be intensified unless specific arrangements are made regarding the

urgent matters outlined above well in advance of May 15, 1948.

In those lapidary sentences the Commission made clear to the civilized world that solely because of the lack of preventive measures that could so easily have been taken, the Palestine plan adopted by the Assembly had not proved worth the paper upon which it had been written; that a new holocaust was about to flame in the Holy Land; that major hostilities, whose end no one could foresee, were now imminent; and that the Security Council had been consistently recalcitrant to its obligations and its responsibilities. This bankruptcy of the Security Council had been due to no Soviet veto. It had been due exclusively to the policies of selfish and short-sighted expediency pursued by Great Britain, and, still more, by the United States.

The delegates to the Assembly were faced with a further accomplished fact, which no amount of legalistic sophistries on the part of the American and British delegates could explain away: partition, as provided by the Assembly's resolution, had already been achieved by Jewish action. The Jews of Palestine, although without the help of the United Nations Commission, had carried out most of the obligations placed upon them by the partition plan. They now announced that upon May 16, the day after the termination of the British mandate, an independent Jewish state in Palestine would be established under a new Jewish central authority. Was it conceivable that the General Assembly, after the Jews had created the foundation for the independent nation promised them by the Assembly's partition plan and had complied with the responsibilities entrusted to them by that plan, could now permit the Jews to be exterminated or driven out from the territory granted them by the aggression of the

Arabs who had defied the will of the Assembly? Was the Assembly, as the United States now demanded, to impose by force upon the Jews a trusteeship which by its terms would deprive them of the very freedom that the Assembly had offered them?

There was certainly no light thrown upon any of the problems before the delegates by the official statements or actions of the United States.

The concrete proposals embodied in Ambassador Austin's suggestion of a trusteeship created a dilemma far greater than that existing before the American abandonment of the partition plan.

The American delegate had stated:

> We believe that further steps must be taken immediately not only to maintain the peace but also to afford a further opportunity to reach an agreement between the interested parties regarding the future government of Palestine. To this end we believe that a temporary trusteeship of Palestine should be established under the Trusteeship Council of the United Nations. Such a United Nations trusteeship would be without prejudice to the rights, claims, or position of the parties concerned, or to the character of the eventual political settlement which we hope can be achieved without long delay. In our opinion the Security Council should recommend the establishment of such a trusteeship to the General Assembly and to the mandatory Power.

The reasons alleged for the abandonment by the United States of the partition plan were: that force would be required in its implementation, that the Security Council had no power to employ force to impose a "political settlement," and that in any event no such force had been established. Where was the force to be obtained "to maintain the peace," as the United States now declared was necessary, when it was only too plain that the force needed to impose a trusteeship upon Palestine would have to be even greater than that needed to impose partition? From what source would the United Nations derive the power to impose a trusteeship upon the Jews and Arabs in Palestine, when both had announced their opposition?

What possible ground could exist for the hope of the United States, as expressed by Ambassador Austin, that the "eventual political settlement" could "be achieved without long delay"?

It was certainly unlikely that the proposals of the United States would receive the approval of the Assembly unless the American Government made a clear-cut commitment that it would bear the chief burden of providing the military force and the money needed to impose and to administer the trusteeship that it now recommended. The assurance contained in President Truman's "explanation" of American policy, "if the United Nations agrees to a temporary trusteeship we must take our share of the necessary responsibility" carried no conviction. How could it when the United States had just reversed the policy to which it had officially committed itself only three months before and when objections vehemently expressed in the American Congress made it obvious that the Congress would not consent to the despatch of American troops to Palestine without its approval?

The delegates were also forced to the unhappy conclusion that the Russo-American contest prevailing in every other part of the world would now extend also to Palestine, and would result in a consistent effort by the Soviet Union to block or to frustrate every measure initiated by the United States on which the remaining members of the United Nations might agree.

The reaction of the Soviet Union to the American

change of policy had been immediate. It had created a profound effect. The Soviet delegate informed the Security Council that his Government reiterated its conviction that "the decision adopted by the General Assembly on the partition of Palestine into two independent – Jewish and Arab – states is a just solution." He further charged:

> If the United States and some other states wreck the implementation of the partition plan and consider Palestine as a component element in their economic, military and strategic calculations, then any decision on the future of Palestine, including the establishment of trusteeship, will mean the transformation of Palestine into a field of dissension and struggle for the Jews and Arabs and will only increase the number of victims.
>
> Full responsibility for the killing of the decision on the partition of Palestine rests on the United States, which, according to general opinion, takes care, not of the just settlement of the question of the future of Palestine and the relations between Arabs and Jews, but of their own oil interests and military-strategic positions in the Middle East. . . . The convening of any special session on the Palestine issue would mean throwing the United Nations backwards at least for a year in regard to the Palestine question, while our task is not that of moving backwards, but of making progress and of implementing the decision already adopted.

A point of view no less categorical was expressed by Doctor Herbert Evatt, the Australian Minister for External Affairs. Doctor Evatt enjoyed a well-deserved and very considerable measure of influence in the Assembly. He had taken an active part in framing the partition plan that the Assembly had recommended. Speaking from Australia for his Government he had said:

> Decisions of a competent international conference should

be accepted after there has been full inquiry and fair debate and a just settlement has been reached. . . . The United Nations decision was reached by more than a two-thirds majority, the only dissentients being the Arab states and certain nations associated very closely with them. The decision was a just and impartial one and must not be lightly set aside. . . . After all that had occurred, to throw the solution into the melting pot again may be very damaging to the authority of the United Nations. It has been contended that the enforcement of the Assembly's decision is not possible. Had the great Powers who supported the proposal at Lake Success adhered firmly to it, there would have been little difficulty. In any event, under the Assembly's decision the new Jewish state and the new Arab state was each to be entitled to establish its own military forces for the defense of the new territory, and this decision clearly carried with it the rights of Jews as well as Arabs to import arms and equipment for the purpose of defense. . . . In my opinion the United Nations' decision has been gradually undermined by intrigues directed against the Jewish people. It would be little short of a tragedy if the fundamental rights of self-government were to be denied to both the Jews and the Arabs as it is guaranteed to them under the Assembly's decision. . . . The only considerations that influenced the United Nations were those of justice and fair dealing to all concerned. It would be most disturbing if mere considerations of power politics or of expediency were allowed to destroy the decision. However, if a Special United Nations Assembly is called, it is hardly likely to accept any plan which involves the annihilation of the previous decision unless new facts of overwhelming cogency are proved to exist. I need hardly add that under the United Nations Charter the Security Council has no power whatever to overrule the recommendation of the Assembly.

Although coming from widely divergent sources, the reactions of the Australian and Soviet Governments expressed the opinions of many members of the United Nations who feared to speak openly.

What in reality could a new Assembly do that the previous Assembly had not done? There was clearly nothing to be gained by further consultations among the member states. There was even less need for any further investigations. If the American proposals were not in fact merely a cover for some secret understanding between the United States and Great Britain, as the Soviet Government charged, concluded for the purpose of imposing a military occupation of the Western Powers upon Palestine, what advantages could be advanced in favor of a trusteeship? If this Special Session of the Assembly were to deal honestly and justly with the issues before it, must it not in all fairness decide that the implementation of partition was less hazardous to the cause of world peace, and far less likely to provoke new international controversies, than an attempt to set up a trusteeship?

President Truman's demand, conveyed through Ambassador Austin to the Security Council, "that representatives of the Arabs and Jews be called at once to the Council table to arrange a truce," could hardly be regarded seriously. It represented a most worthy aspiration. But it was painfully unrealistic. The violence in Palestine had increased to such a degree that the holy places were in grave danger. Fanaticism was predominant. Passions were out of control. The bitterness between the Jews and Arabs was becoming hourly more intense. Similar appeals offered earlier under far more favorable auspices had been wholly disregarded. It seemed a foregone conclusion that no appeal for a truce would now be heeded, and that no responsible Jewish or Arab leaders would agree to consult.

And so it proved. As the Assembly met, the Security

Council remained in session to adopt a resolution demanding that the Jews and Arabs in Palestine immediately accept a truce. The terms of the resolution were heavily loaded against the Jews. There was no demand on the part of the Council that the armed bands of Arabs who had invaded Palestine from neighboring countries withdraw. The Arabs had already declared that they would accept a truce only if they were given binding assurances that partition had been abandoned. The Jews expressed their willingness to agree to a truce only if they received equally binding assurances from the United Nations that the decision upon partition remained unaltered. Moreover, could the Jews of Palestine reasonably be expected to accept a truce unless they obtained a commitment from the United Nations that the Arab invaders would be forced to withdraw, and that the arms that they themselves were not permitted to receive would no longer be made available to their opponents? It was hardly surprising that both Jews and Arabs flatly rejected the Council's demand. But with this refusal the authority of the Council further decreased.

Many well-intentioned proposals came from unofficial sources. The appeal of religious leaders that Jerusalem be considered an "open city," guaranteed against attack, was, of course, fully justified. But far too many of these proposals were wholly partisan in their nature; others seemed again altogether to overlook the gravity of the situation in Palestine and the strength of the human passions that had been aroused. They were predicated upon the belief that an appeal to reason would still be sufficient, or upon a bland unwillingness to see that only force exercised by the United Nations could prove effective if complete disaster was still to be averted.

One proposal which seemed to envisage only the interests of the Arabs was advanced by a group of prominent citizens under the chairmanship of Dean Virginia C. Gildersleeve. The gist of this proposal was that "the Palestine problem must be solved through conciliation, or some sort of compromise agreed to by both the Arabs and the Jews." No more suitable reply to such suggestions could have been made than the statement of James G. MacDonald. Mr. MacDonald, who had for many years contributed, in various official capacities, toward the solution of the international refugees' problem, who had represented the United States during the period immediately prior to the War in negotiations designed to save the lives of the Jews of Nazi Germany, and who had served as a member of the Anglo-American Committee of Inquiry on Palestine, pointed out that the proposal of the Gildersleeve Committee was

> tantamount to asking the Jews to surrender their hopes and their rights in Palestine. The Arab leaders, when they appeared to give testimony before the Anglo-American Committee of Inquiry, were unanimous and unyielding in their demand that the Jews should relinquish all special rights, or claims to such rights, in Palestine. . . . In short, the Arab spokesmen would agree to nothing less than that the Jews become a helpless and defenseless minority in their historic, and promised, Homeland. In the two years since the Anglo-American Committee concluded its hearings, Arab intransigence had not diminished. Instead, if that were possible, it had increased.
>
> In view of this Arab defiance, the call of the Committee for a "compromise" agreeable to both the Jews and the Arabs must have the effect of bringing pressure to bear upon the Jews to yield to Arab intransigence. How such pressure can contribute towards "peace and justice in the Holy Land" is a mystery which neither the Committee's

statement nor the explanation of its Chairman does anything to clear up.

The proposals tentatively offered by the United States for the consideration of the Assembly bore however, regrettably enough, a close resemblance, in their inspiration, to the recommendations of the Gildersleeve Committee. The American suggestions were for a "temporary," although indefinite, trusteeship, to continue until Jews and Arabs had agreed on a future government of Palestine; for an elected legislature in which the Jews would be a minority, and for the subordination of further Jewish immigration and the sale of land to Jews to an agreement between Arabs and Jews, which of course meant that Jewish immigration and land purchases would be halted; and finally, for the relegation of the policing of Palestine to members of the United Nations capable of supplying and financing the armed forces required, these member states to be designated in advance.

What all this implied was that the Jews would thereby be definitely deprived of the hope of independence; that no refuge in Palestine could be offered more than a handful of Europe's refugees; and that while no force could be found for the imposition of partition, force could be found – presumably by Great Britain, France and the United States – for the imposition of a trusteeship that would satisfy the strategic and economic requirements of the American Government.

To those who had long maintained that because of the growing contest between the West and the East, every requirement of far-sighted statesmanship demanded a rapid settlement of the Palestine controversy so that Palestine might not become a new field for Soviet-American rivalry, these American proposals, quite apart from their flagrant injustice, gave cause for the gravest concern.

It was said in Washington that since the Soviet Union had refused to participate in the Trusteeship Council the Soviet Union could, therefore, have no part in a Palestine trusteeship were the Assembly to adopt the American recommendations. It was true that Russia had appointed no representative upon the Trusteeship Council. But her adherence was a matter for her own determination. The Charter of the United Nations stipulates that any trusteeship plan proposed by the Trusteeship Council must secure, before it becomes effective, the agreement of all "directly interested" nations. Were the United States to claim a "direct interest" in a Palestine trusteeship it would be inconceivable that a similar "direct interest" would not be claimed by the Soviet Union, which could legitimately claim that Russia's interests were far more directly affected by what went on in Palestine, than were those of the United States, a Power geographically altogether remote.

And this is precisely what occurred. On April 25, 1948, the Soviet Government ended its boycott of the Trusteeship Council. It named Semyon Tsarapkin its delegate to fill the seat in the Council to which Russia as a major Power was entitled under the Charter, and which had been empty for thirteen months. While no veto right exists in the Trusteeship Council, Russia would thus have the opportunity to make herself heard before any decision could be reached either on the nature of the proposed Trusteeship or on the composition of the forces to be sent to impose it. The American maneuver was thus quickly shown to be as futile as it had been foolish.

From the standpoint of power politics, in which the Soviet Union and the United States were now engaged, could it be doubted, if the United States undertook, directly or indirectly, to control Palestine, and to send there either its own troops or those of its Western allies, that the Soviet Union would not either seek to prevent it, or else, as a means of strategic defense, present Greece, Turkey, and Iran with a demand for the conclusion of "military alliances" that would secure for the Soviet Union an equivalent access to the Eastern Mediterranean and to the oil resources of the Near East?

In the light of all of the contingencies existing as the Assembly met on April 16, the abandonment by the United States of the partition plan seemed even more fantastically short-sighted.

But the relentless influence upon the policies of other nations that American policy under present world conditions is bound to have, made it unlikely, even if the Assembly were to refuse to abandon it, that the partition plan could still be carried out unless there was a new reversal of American policy with regard to Palestine.

That is the basic difficulty in trying to answer the question, What can still be done?

A truce is imperative if carnage is to be prevented, if the holy places are to be spared, if all of the achievements of the Jews in Palestine are not to be obliterated, and if the United Nations is not to become a subject for scorn and a hollow sham. But no real truce can be expected if its terms deny the Jews their ultimate freedom or if it condemns the pitiful Jewish refugees in Europe to continued exclusion from Palestine.

International recognition should be granted the provisional government of the Jewish state as soon as it is constituted in accordance with the provisions of the partition plan under whose authority the Jews have set it up. Certainly the Palestine Commission, established by the resolution of November 29, 1947, should be authorized to continue as the Assembly's agent in Palestine, and certainly the Jews of Palestine should be permitted, under the supervision of the Commission, to obtain from the United States the arms they need for self-defense, until law and order have been restored in Palestine. But none of these steps can be more than mere palliatives.

In April the King of Trans-Jordan and the Governments of the other adjacent Arab States had announced their intention of invading Palestine as soon as the British mandate should terminate on May 15. The Jewish forces seized the great port of Haifa after defeating its Arab defenders. Doctor Ben-Gurion became Prime Minister of the new Jewish state, and announced the intention of the Jews to defend their territory at all costs.

Mr. Bevin, Britain's Foreign Secretary, again told the House of Commons that the British mandate would end on May 15, no matter what may transpire, and that no British troops would be available to prevent Arab aggression in Palestine after that date.

The Trusteeship Council finally designated the French, Belgian, and American Consuls in Jerusalem as a Truce Commission to try to persuade the Jews and Arabs to agree to a temporary truce within the walled city of the ancient capital. In the state of open anarchy then prevailing in Jerusalem it is not surprising that the pleas of the Truce Commission had no immediate practical results.

In the first days of May, press correspondents reported the despatch to the frontiers of Palestine of regular troops from Iraq, Trans-Jordan, and Egypt. The Truce Commission displayed sufficient initiative to send a telegram to King Abdullah of Trans-Jordan warning him in the name of the United Nations "to abstain from any military decisions or acts." Whatever deterrent effect this may have had was at once negatived by the Security Council when it publicly announced that, inasmuch as the Arab Governments had "not yet done anything," there was no reason for the Council to send them any warning.

And in the Political Committee of the Assembly, bogged down in an endless number of legalistic debates over the American Trusteeship proposals, the sole American contribution toward the prevention of the impending calamity was the reassuring declaration of the American representative that "the position of the United States is very clear and simple."

In the despairing confusion into which every agency of the United Nations had been plunged as a result of American policy, only one realistic note was heard. It came from Pablo Azcarate who had been sent to Palestine as an advance agent of the United Nations Palestine Commission and who returned to report on April 29. Señor Azcarate informed the Commission that the Jewish administration in the areas allotted by the partition plan to the Jewish state was complete; that partition was already an accomplished fact; that all that was lacking was legal recognition of a condition that existed, and of a condition that would continue to exist unless the United Nations permitted it to be obliterated by the Arab troops massing on Palestine's frontiers.

In early May it became apparent that if a Trusteeship was imposed it would mean the subjugation by force of the Jews who were for the first time experiencing the sensation of independence. Unless the United Nations, however, were to intervene in their behalf it seemed improbable that they could long exercise that independence if they were attacked by the greatly superior regular armies of the Arab countries.

There can be no hope for peace in Palestine, other

than peace by extermination, unless the partition plan adopted by the Assembly six months ago is reinstated as the definitive expression of its decision, and unless that plan, backed by an adequate armed force established by the United Nations, once more receives the official support of the United States.

9

Palestine and the Future of the United Nations

IN ANY ATTEMPT to appraise our Palestine policy fairly and objectively these two questions must be answered. Have this Government's policies been justified on the ground of national security? Have these policies strengthened the United Nations and thereby made it more likely that we will eventually have a world order under which this nation can prosper and be secure?

Granted the contest between the Soviet Union and the Western Powers, it is a matter of cardinal importance to this country to preserve peace in the Eastern Mediterranean, and to prevent any developments that might facilitate Soviet expansion in that area. Has American policy been calculated to further the attainment of those two objectives?

A strategic consideration that has been uppermost in the minds of the policy-makers in Washington has been the question of Near Eastern oil. Those who are directly responsible for the reversal of our Palestine policy tell us that the oil produced in the Near East must be available to the countries of Western Europe if the European Recovery Program is to succeed, and that the oil resources available to us are so depleted that Near Eastern oil is indispensable if we have to take part in a new war.

Taken by themselves, there is much in these assertions that is not open to contradiction. But when they are used as a justification for the reversal of this nation's declared policy, the individual citizen is entitled to subject them to careful analysis.

Should the present tension between the Soviet Union and the Western Powers result in hostilities, what reason have we to assume that the United States or any other Western Power could still have access to this oil? The existing British military forces in the Near East, even if the United States were able to re-enforce them quickly, could hardly prevent the Soviet Union from rapidly occupying Iran and Iraq, and from thereby securing these countries' oil resources as well as control of the air over the rest of the oil-producing areas of the Near East. Even though the American plan for a Palestine Trusteeship may envisage the utilization of Palestine as a base for the air and ground forces of the Western democracies, it is improbable that those forces could prevent the success of a major effort by the Soviet Union to occupy Mesopotamia and Arabia. It might well be that later on the United States and its Allies, if they kept control of North and East Africa, could recapture these areas from the Russians. But certainly by then the oil wells and their equipment would have been wrecked and rendered unproductive.

We also hear from the same sources that had the United States continued to support the partition plan the hostility of the Arabs would have been so great that they would have been more likely to respond to Soviet inducements, and that the Arabs would in any case have abrogated the American oil concessions.

Since the Soviet Union from the outset consistently supported the partition plan, there was no reason to suppose that the Arabs would acquiesce in Russian support for partition while they at the same time broke with the United States because it also supported partition. It was equally unrealistic to assume that Arab Governments such as those of Iraq and of Saudi Arabia, which chiefly depend upon their oil royalties, would voluntarily deprive themselves of these indispensable revenues when no other way of cashing in on their oil resources was open to them.

Our defense authorities have also told us that if the United States had persisted in its support for the partition plan, after the United Nations became convinced that force would be needed to implement it, the Soviet Union would have insisted upon sending Russian troops to Palestine, and that in that event further Soviet expansion into Arabia and into the Mediterranean would have become a certainty.

The calamitous failure of the United States to obtain through the Security Council, when the partition plan was adopted by the Assembly in November, 1947, the creation of a United Nations force to keep the peace in Palestine until partition had been carried out, has made it much harder to establish some kind of a United Nations constabulary that would be free from Soviet participation. But there is as yet no valid reason to suppose that a constabulary composed of contingents from small Powers having no direct interest in Palestine could not still be established without incurring a Soviet veto. It was in fact hoped by many of the smaller countries, when the Assembly met on April 16, 1948, that should the United States obtain approval for its Trusteeship proposal, it would recommend just such a force to impose it.

It was clear that if the United States maintained its apparent intention of having a trusteeship over Palestine sustained by forces of the United States, Great Britain and France, there could be no question as to the nature of the Soviet reaction.

Our policy-makers, in their plans of global strategy, seemed to be assuming that by abandoning partition they would win the loyal support for the United States and its Western Allies of the Arab world. Great Britain has for many generations tried to obtain that support. She has catered to Arab ambitions and to Arab prejudices. She has continued heavily to subsidize Arab Governments at times when she could ill afford it. Yet the history of the past three decades demonstrates conclusively that when Arab leaders have believed that their own interest would thereby be better served they have usually defaulted in their obligations to Great Britain. The Iraqi revolt in the spring of 1941, when the fate of Great Britain hung in the balance, backed though it may have been by Nazi agents, was a genuine Arab movement. The persistent attempt of the Grand Mufti of Jerusalem to help the Axis defeat the British, and to obtain control of the Near East, was widely supported, and is even today enthusiastically endorsed, in many Arab countries.

The notorious Syrian, Fawzi Bey Kawkji, now playing a leading part in the Arab aggressions in Palestine, was in German pay during the time he served as the Mufti's chief guerrilla leader in the Arab revolt in 1936, and fled from Palestine with the Mufti in 1939. He was a key figure in the Iraqi revolt of 1941. He was in Berlin conspiring with the Nazi leaders during the later period of the war. He has recently been a prime director in the resistance of the Arab Higher Committee to the United Nations.

It is true that the British Foreign Office still hopes for

an alliance with the members of the Arab League as a means of securing British interests and of checking Russian penetration. But it is surely wishful thinking on our part to imagine that in any conflict between the West and the East the Arab countries would support the Western cause if the inducements from the other side seemed at any moment to be more tempting.

By using all of our influence to prevent the birth of an independent Jewish Commonwealth in Palestine we have been, however, preventing the creation of the one Near Eastern state that would prove to be a true democracy, and a democracy that, because of the manner of being of its people, as well as because of their own self-interest, would unquestionably be an unswerving supporter of the Western cause.

The attempt has recently been rather successfully made by Arab leaders, notably by Faris El-Khouri, the Syrian representative on the Security Council, to persuade the American public that were a Jewish state now to be set up, it would be overwhelmingly Communist in its sympathies and a willing tool of the Kremlin. Stories are recurrent that recent groups of refugees have been packed with Soviet agents. We are told that the Jewish resistance forces are led by Soviet officers.

Undoubtedly Soviet agents are in Palestine. Wherever there is unrest, wherever there are social or racial disputes, the communist conspirators will "horn in." They are doing it in our own country. But it must be remembered that the economic structure which the Jews set up in Palestine under the British mandate is wholly anti-communist in its nature. The Jewish communal agricultural colonies in Palestine are co-operatives, in which the prevailing spirit is fiercely democratic. Jewish industries are privately owned. At the present moment an overwhelming majority of the Palestine Jews are vehemently anti-communist in their political beliefs, and would resist as intolerable any attempt by the Soviet Union upon their individual liberties. The leadership within the Jewish Agency has consistently based its policy upon the West, and in recent times more particularly upon the United States. The executive of the Jewish Agency represents a coalition of left of center and of conservative labor groups.

Judging from recent authoritative surveys not more than four per cent of the Jewish population of Palestine follows the banner of the hammer and sickle. The only representative that the communist groups had in the Jewish Agency, Moshe Sneh, resigned in January 1948 because he believed, notwithstanding the support Russia gave to partition, that partition would make less likely any close link in the future between Moscow and Jerusalem.

The abandonment by the United States of the partition plan gravely weakened the political prestige of the leaders of the democratic majority, and correspondingly increased the influence of the communists. The latter are now alleging that had the Jewish Agency sought the support of the Soviet Union rather than that of the United States, they would have fared far better. A great number of Jews are persuaded that the United States has "sold them out" to the Arabs, and the impact of American policy upon the political future of the Palestinian Jews may be disastrous. The United States has materially reduced the chances for the construction of a Near Eastern bulwark of Western democracy, and has thereby lessened the likelihood that many of the very strategic advantages that it hoped to secure by abandoning partition can now be won.

In this appraisal of the effects of our Palestine policy

upon our national security, it must be borne uppermost in mind that in the determination of what makes for the security of the United States there is far more to be taken into account than economic or military considerations alone. This country's security is necessarily affected by factors that, while less tangible, are for that reason no less important.

The explanation given by Secretary Marshall that our reversal was due "to vital elements of our national security" had reference to the more tangible considerations. The Administration apparently failed to realize that by this reversal the United States was awakening suspicion in the minds of governments and of peoples throughout the world that it was not only following no consistent and firm foreign policy, but that it was also willing to welch on its commitments should those commitments seem to it to involve new hazards or new burdens.

At the very moment when the United States was seeking to rally the countries of Western Europe to American leadership in the face of Russian expansion, the United States adopted a course which shook confidence in this country throughout the world. There was never a time when the confidence of other peoples in the dependability of this nation represented a more vital element of our national security.

The immediate effect upon the confidence of the small nations in this country's leadership could not be better illustrated than by the declaration of the representative of a Latin-American Republic when the American reversal on partition was announced: "First they convinced us that partition was the only answer. Now they are trying to convince us that partition is insane. It is true that I represent a small nation which cannot stand alone. I am willing to accept United States leadership. But this is treachery. By this latest reversal the United States has forfeited whatever moral justification it once had for leading the small nations."

It is also in this broader sense that our recent policy, because it has so gravely impaired the authority and prestige of the United Nations, has further weakened this nation's security.

In the early autumn of 1947, before the Assembly adopted its resolution for the economic union and partition of Palestine, the faith that the average man and woman had placed in the United Nations had begun to crumble. Antagonism between the Soviet Union and the Western Powers had been crippling the United Nations. Russian objections had impeded the establishment of the International Police Force which the Council must have if it is to carry out its obligations. Russian obduracy had prevented any agreement for the international control of the atomic bomb. Not only had no start yet been made in disarmament, but both Russia and the United States were rapidly rearming. The use by the Soviet Union of its veto power had made it impossible for the Security Council to take action that was necessary if new conflicts were to be prevented.

The masses of the people later saw, however, that the Assembly had, by a substantial majority, agreed upon a fair and practicable settlement for one of the most controversial problems of modern times. They had also seen that the Soviet Union and the United States both supported the agreement reached, and that the effects of power politics would therefore not be likely to prevent the United Nations from taking at least this one long step toward the construction of a stable world order.

What was more than ever necessary was that popular

confidence in the United Nations, and international respect for its authority, be revived by a concrete demonstration that the United Nations could work, and that it had the power needed to make its will prevail. A successful implementation of the Palestine plan would have heartened peoples in every part of the world. It would have done much to rally support for the United Nations at a critical moment in its existence. And it must be plain to all of us that because of the obstacles which it will for some time continue to encounter as a consequence of the contest between the East and the West, the United Nations must have the support and the confidence of popular opinion at this moment if it is eventually to succeed or even to survive.

Yet it was that very moment that the United States selected to demand that the power of the United Nations be curtailed and that it show itself before the world as helpless to enforce its will.

When the Charter of the United Nations was first conceived, it was intended that the Security Council should function as the executive Power. It was to be the sole United Nations agency to be entrusted with the authority to employ force to restrain aggressors and to maintain peace. But it was further envisaged as an agency that would, on behalf of all of the United Nations, have the power, through methods of persuasion, conciliation, or negotiation, or even through the imposition of political settlements, to remove the causes for aggression and war.

As the Secretary General of the United Nations pointed out in his legal opinion of January 10, 1947, concerning the statute of Trieste, the records of the San Francisco Conference, where the United Nations Charter was adopted, show that all of the delegations that then expressed their views "recognized that the authority of the

Council was not restricted" to the specific powers conferred upon it by those chapters of the Charter that prescribe the Council's obligations and rights.

The Secretary General stated:

> It was recognized in this discussion that the responsibility to maintain peace and security carried with it a power to discharge that responsibility. This power, it was noted, was not unlimited, but subject to the purposes and principles of the United Nations.
>
> It is apparent that this discussion reflects a basic conception of the Charter, namely, that the members of the United Nations have conferred upon the Security Council powers commensurate with its responsibility for the maintenance of peace and security. The only limitations are those fundamental principles and purposes found in Chapter 1 of the Charter.

Under this broad construction of the powers of the Security Council, strongly supported by the United States at that time, the claim now made by this Government that the Security Council has no power to carry out the Assembly's plan for the partition of Palestine, falls by the board. If this restrictive interpretation demanded by the United States is upheld by the other member states, the United Nations will be deprived of all authority to eliminate, save by persuasion, the causes for war, and the United Nations to that extent will be rendered impotent.

On September 18, 1931, Japan occupied by military force strategic areas in southern Manchuria.

Three days later China appealed for help to the League of Nations. During the following two months the Council of the League of Nations took no action other than the adoption of two pallid resolutions. To a great majority of the American people Japan's aggression against China was none of our business. While they had refused to assume any of the responsibilities involved in membership in the League of Nations, they insisted that it was the League's business to take action, and that their Government should "stay out of it." The most that a far-sighted American Secretary of State, Henry L. Stimson, could do was to announce, in the name of the United States, that this country would not recognize the gains that Japan might secure by her aggression. When he requested the co-operation of the British Government, this was refused.

For reasons which seemed to them then to be reasons of "prudent" expediency, the other major Powers that were members of the League refused to consider military sanctions against Japan. Even a resort to economic sanctions was vetoed. Japan was permitted unscathed to walk out of the League of Nations, and to continue unhampered her southward march through China.

As a result, the peace machinery established by the League of Nations broke down. The cause of collective security received a blow from which it has never recovered.

There could not have been more than a handful of men in the autumn of 1931 who saw with any clarity what the ultimate outcome of all this must be. Yet the events which had their origin in that failure of statesmanship, in that short-sighted selfishness, and in that preoccupation with alleged expediency, on the part of those who were then directing the destinies of the democracies, led inexorably to the Second World War and to the attack on Pearl Harbor.

While there is still time we should recognize the parallel that must be drawn between the issue presented by the invasion of Manchuria seventeen years ago, and the issue presented by the refusal of the United States to face the risks involved in the imposition of the partition plan for Palestine.

For reasons that it claimed were reasons of expediency, the United States abandoned the plan for the settlement of the Palestine problem approved by the Assembly of the United Nations, which it had itself declared was both just and the best calculated to make for peace. It reversed its own policy in the face of an Arab invasion of Palestine, and in the face of armed resistance by the Arab states to the authority of the United Nations.

Can there be any truer verdict rendered upon American policy than that which is found in the address delivered by Sir Carl Berendsen, the delegate of New Zealand, when the American proposals for Trusteeship came before the Assembly on April 20, 1948:

> The Assembly in its November decision did the right thing, but by reason of its failure to provide for implementation, it did the right thing in the wrong way, and because of our error then, we have the situation today. The result of our error is death, bloodshed, murder, outrage and agony in Palestine. The result of our error then is a grave risk that the Assembly of the United Nations is in serious and humiliating danger of losing the public confidence upon which its authority in the last resort depends. . . . If partition with economic union was right in November, it is right today, and indeed I have heard no logical suggestion to the contrary. The circumstances have not changed in the slightest.
>
> The only new factor that has arisen is a detestable series of murders and outrages in Palestine. . . . It is now suggested . . . that because of this series of murders and outrages, partition at this stage has become impossible. . . . To put them forward as a reason for abandoning the decision arrived at after most careful and anxious consideration only

> a few months ago seems to the New Zealand delegation to be a most fantastic distortion of logical thought. . . . If the members of the United Nations should be willing each to take its proportionate part in enforcing a decision of the United Nations in respect of a Trusteeship for Palestine, those members should, on any logical basis, equally be willing to provide their proportionate share of a United Nations force to implement the decision to which it pledged itself last November.
>
> I call upon my colleagues to take careful thought before they strike that tragic, perhaps irreparable, blow to the United Nations that would be involved in capitulation by the world to threats and violence.
>
> Here is a test case, and believe me, the future of the organization, and the future of the world may indeed depend upon the way in which it is decided.

In the proposals for Trusteeship which it urged upon the other members of the United Nations as a substitute for the partition plan, the United States included provisions which would deprive the Jews of Palestine of any hope of independence, and which would bar the entrance into Palestine of all but a handful of the Jewish refugees of Europe. It urged the establishment of a precedent which would place a premium upon aggression, and upon a successful defiance of the authority of the United Nations.

If the United States persists in the course upon which it then embarked, what hope can there be for collective security?

If we look behind the screen of legalistic verbiage with which spokesmen for our Government have surrounded the issue of Palestine, and see the fundamentals as they are, the true reason for the abandonment by the United States of the partition plan is that it feared its execution would have involved some added burdens and some risks.

It was exactly that same reason that caused Great Britain and France in 1931 to refuse to agree to effective action by the League of Nations against Japan.

We have made it plain that just as the great Powers wrecked the League of Nations by using it as an instrument of their own national policy, and by fulfilling their obligations to the cause of collective security only when it suited their own selfish national convenience, so we are now using the United Nations as an instrument of our own national policy, and fulfilling our obligations to the cause of collective security only when that seems to serve our own selfish and national ends.

The policy of the United States in the case of Palestine has been devoid of vision and devoid of principle.

It has been devoid of principle in that justice and the struggle for freedom of a bitterly afflicted people have been prostituted to the shabby exigencies of local politics and of powerful domestic interests, and subordinated to the influence of militarism.

It has been devoid of vision in that the cause of collective security, by whose triumph alone the United States can insure its lasting safety, has been sacrificed to short-sighted and selfish expediency.

The two world wars have left behind them a measure of human suffering which cannot yet be fully comprehended. The mark which they have left upon our civilization will not for generations be obliterated. Uncounted millions of men and women have placed their hopes in the capacity of their leaders to build a new and better world.

"It is through suffering that learning comes."

How much more suffering must humanity endure before it finally learns to put the whole before the part; to understand that only in the safety of the community of the nations can any nation find its own safety?

At this climactic moment in history the future destinies of Western civilization rest in the hands of the American people. If we will only see that when our Government weakens the structure of collective security it thereby weakens our capacity to help to build a new world order under which this nation can safely live, and under which all peoples can advance toward freedom and security, we need not fail to meet the challenge that Fate has offered us.

THE END

Index